The
Golf Doctor

The
Golf Doctor
First aid for your game

Edward Craig

BB Bounty
Books

For my Family and Tidelines

First published in Great Britain in 2004 by
Hamlyn, a division of Octopus Publishing Group Ltd

This edition published in 2008 by Bounty Books,
a division of Octopus Publishing Group Ltd
2–4 Heron Quays, London E14 4JP

An Hachette Livre UK Company
www.hachettelivre.co.uk

Copyright © Octopus Publishing Group Ltd 2004

ISBN 978-0-753710-41-8

A CIP catalogue record for this book is available from the
British Library

Printed and bound in China

Publisher's note
The text has been written from the point-of-view of
teaching a right-handed player. Reverse the advice given for
left-handed players to read 'left' for 'right' and vice versa.

Contents

Introduction

Golf can be a terrifying sport to take up – from finding the right equipment to braving your first course and clubhouse. The real terror starts, though, once you have bought yourself a set of clubs and started getting the ball airborne as you then see where you are going wrong. Surviving golf's vagaries and frustrations is part of the enjoyment of the sport, but it's best to avoid trying to convince a golfer of this after they've sliced into the water. The highs that follow the lows make golf the addictive and engaging sport that keeps millions enthralled.

The Golf Doctor aims to help your game by cutting through the quagmire of jargon-ridden instruction and offering simple advice to simple queries. If your rounds are consistently being ruined by fluffed chip shots or weak drives from every tee, then *The Golf Doctor* will help you find the cure.

For many people, mystery, austerity and pomposity shroud golf. Thankfully, the likes of Tiger Woods, Sergio Garcia and Annika Sorenstam are opening it up to millions.

They are showing the sport for what it really is: a fantastic, infuriating, unconquerable and addictive game. As old-fashioned ways disappear, so does the mystery of how best to play.

The Golf Doctor is an on-course reference guide that offers clear and concise advice on how to treat the ills that plague your game. If you slice severely from the first three tees, you don't want any complicated theory; you just want it to stop. With the simple on-course tips, thoughts and drills that you will find in this book, you can patch up and rescue your round. The more permanent solutions in these pages will help your game in the long term.

The fun of golf can be lost if you play consistently badly, with particular parts of your game always letting you down. Here you will find simple answers to treat specific problems immediately, just what the Doctor ordered.

Edward Craig

How to use this book

The Golf Doctor is designed to provide every golfer with an easy diagnosis and remedy for their on-course problems, together with suggestions for permanent cures. There are few things worse for a golfer than discovering a problem with their game but being stuck in the middle of a round with only a know-it-all partner to offer advice on their golfing gaffes. This book is designed to give you a better source of advice and will help aid recovery from any golfing malady. It is divided into seven sections, each dealing with a different aspect of the game. All you have to do is identify your problem, find it in the appropriate section and then follow four steps to cure it completely.

Step one

The symptoms

In golf, as with a medical problem, you will be suffering from symptoms. If you have a health problem you go to the doctor, who will ask you what is wrong so that he can provide the best diagnosis. You must be candid and talk openly. With golf, it is the same. You have to admit freely your problems to find the cure for them. If you have a slice, admit it – do not pretend that your affliction is a power-fade.

The first step is to turn to the Symptom Chart. This is an initial consultation and it will identify the basic symptoms of any problem. The book is broken down into seven different areas of the game so that you can select the area where you are having trouble: Off the Tee; From the Fairway; Short Game; Putting; Hazards; Course Management; Practice and Equipment. The chart will then guide you through to the Diagnosis.

Step two

The diagnoses

When you have found the diagnosis, you will be asked more specifically about the problem. Are you struggling more with long-irons than short, for instance?

Once you have diagnosed yourself, you can either turn to the on-course First Aid – step three – if you are in desperate need of a quick remedy, or you can look to undertake a long-term recovery – step four.

Step three

On-course first aid

This provides instant answers. Each piece of on-course first aid is designed to be used on the course without major disruption to the rest of your game. The on-course first aid in this book provides technical checks and adjustments and even some easy practice drills that you can try while you are waiting for your turn to play.

The remedies should give you the tools to attack, with renewed confidence, the situations you are finding tricky.

Step four

Long-term recovery

This is the more weighty advice that requires time and energy to practise and absorb. It is often geared around particular drills, to be carried out either on the putting green or on the range. The long-term recovery tips come in the form of intricate drills or specific swing changes, but still provide very digestible advice.

The key is not to overcomplicate the solutions. Often, the simplest advice can make all the difference, and this is what *The Golf Doctor* offers.

Symptom chart

Have a look at the chart that flows over these pages. By following its simple steps, you will easily be able to see any symptoms from which your game is suffering. Once you have established this, follow the references to the diagnoses pages, where there will be a more in-depth analysis of any particular problem. From these sections, you can find either on-course first aid or long-term treatments for golfing ailments.

Where is the problem?

Off the tee	read below
From the fairway	read below
Short game	p11
Hazards	p12
Other problems	p13

Do you have trouble from...?

The tee	see below left
The fairway	see below right

Off the tee
Are you...?

Hitting right	pp14 and 15
Hitting left	pp16 and 17
Catching the top of the ball	p18
Hitting ground before ball	p19
Inconsistent	p20
Missing right and left	p20
Weak off the tee	p21
Hitting high but not far	p21

From the fairway
Are you...?

Not getting the ball airborne	p44
Hitting too much ground	p45
Hitting the ball straight right	p46
Having trouble from bad lies	p47
Inaccurate from hillside lies	p48
Inaccurate from up and down slopes	p49
Wild from the fairway	p50
Inconsistent from the fairway	p51

Where is the problem?

Chipping
Are you...?

Short game
Are you having trouble...?

Putting
Are you...?

Where is the problem?

Bunkers
Are you...?

Hazards
Do you have trouble out of...?

Rough
Are you...?

Where is the problem?

Other problems
Do you have difficulty...?

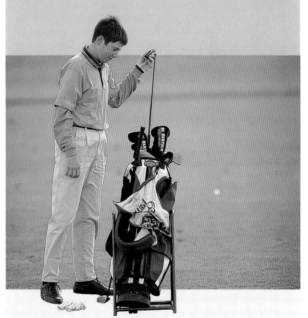

Problem situations
Are you...?

Effective practice
Are you...?

Equipment trauma
Are you...?

Slicing the ball

Every golfer has watched the ball disappear into the rough on the right at some point in their golfing lives. Slicing the ball is the sport's most common problem and accounts for the greatest number of dropped shots.

There are two types of shots that go right – a 'slice' or a 'push' – and they come from separate swing faults. A slice will start on target then curve viciously into trouble – it is an ominous feeling to watch the ball go straight and then, after 18m (20yd), see a slice take hold and land you in the rough.

What causes the slice?

A slice results from an open clubface – aligned right of the target – combined with an out-to-in swing path. When the club starts outside the ball-to-target line and cuts across this line, it has swung 'out-to-in'. The open clubface delivers a glancing blow to the ball, giving it sidespin and curving the ball right. Imagine slicing a tennis ball with a tennis racket. The same thing happens with the golf club and golf ball. It is just harder to spot. The slice spin that you put on the ball will lose distance, so this is a weak shot and will not fly either far or straight.

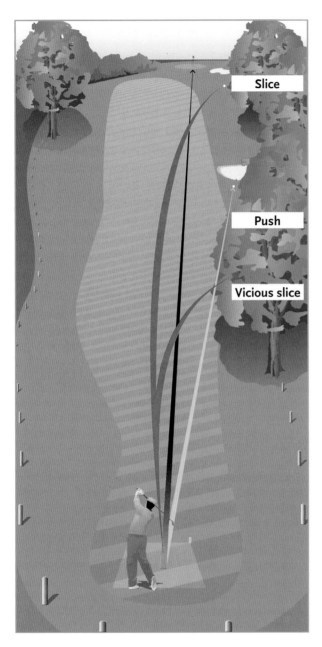

Slice

Push

Vicious slice

There are a number of different ways in which you can lose the ball out to the right. If the ball flies straight and to the right with no curl, then this is a push. If the ball curves right, then you are slicing it. Pushing and slicing the ball not only have different causes but have differing degrees of how problematic they can be for your game.

On-course first aid and long-term recovery

FIXES	GO TO PAGE
● Set-up check for all slicing	p22
● Vicious and wild slices	p23
● The occasional slice	p24
● How to destroy your slice forever	p39

Pushing the ball right

There is the slice, which is very common and very easy to do, and there is the less common push, where the ball disappears straight right. You will feel hard done by when you push the ball because it is likely that you will have made contact with the ball cleanly with the middle of the club, only to see it fly straight right.

A push comes from an entirely different fault from a slice even though the results are similar. A push is the result of your shoulders being aligned right even though the rest of your body is positioned perfectly. The good thing about a push is that the ball travels further through the air, it feels better from the face of the club and is less likely to land you in the wild stuff.

A push flies straight right and will travel further than a slice.

The cause of a slice: the black line shows the ideal ball-to-target line, the blue line is the swing-path and the red line reveals the resulting slice.

✚ On-course first aid and long-term recovery

FIXES	GO TO PAGE
● Set-up check for the push	p26
● Pushing the ball right	p29
● The occasional push	p28
● Bad workman or bad tools?	p124
● Get rid of your push forever	p40

Hooking the ball

If you are not losing balls because of a slice, you may still be losing balls by hooking the ball high and to the left. A hook can be one of the more destructive shots in golf because it travels over a considerable distance before disappearing into some inevitable hazard or leaving you a stroll across three fairways.

A hook starts straight down the middle then veers violently left after travelling 46m (50yd), hits firm ground and bounds on into the rough.

What causes the hook?

The opposite swing flaws to a slice cause a hook – you swing on an in-to-out path and at impact your clubface is closed, or aiming left of the target. This puts topspin on the ball that curves it left.

✚ On-course first aid and long-term recovery

FIXES	GO TO PAGE
● Set-up check for the hooks	p26
● Vicious and wild hooks	p27
● The occasional hook	p28
● Destroy hooks forever	p40

With a hook, the clubhead wraps around the ball in a similar way to a tennis player's topspin forehand.

A hook can be a more destructive shot than a slice as it travels further once it lands.

Pulling the ball

A pull is not as destructive as a hook but it can be particularly irritating because you will make clean contact with the ball only to see it go straight to the left. Sometimes, a pull is the result of over-compensating for a slice. You may find that in order to avoid slicing the ball again to the right you aim left, probably at some trees or water and, to your horror, your ball drops straight into the problem area. A pull is usually not as wild as a hook but it is frustrating that an attempt at a straight shot turns out to be so badly aimed.

On-course first aid and long-term recovery

FIXES	GO TO PAGE
● Set-up check for the pull	p22
● Occasional pulling	p25
● Regular pulling	p25
● Get rid of the pull forever	p38

A pull will disappear straight left and may occur after you've hit a number of balls right.

Pulling the ball is caused by swinging across the ball-to-target line with a square, not open, clubface.

Topping the ball

There is no way round the fact that it is humiliating when you top the ball. You look clumsy and the ball trickles just a few yards off the tee. The one saving grace of topping the ball is that it almost always does not go far enough to land you in any real trouble.

Golfers often hit the ball well on the range, but place them under pressure, with a few people watching, and they'll crack. For this reason, more people top the ball from the first tee than on any other part of the course.

You top the ball when the bottom of the club, as opposed to its face, hits the top half of the ball. The ball then either dribbles off the tee or shoots low and not very far forward. The four main reasons for topping are:

1 Gripping too tightly.

2 Having your legs too straight at address.

3 The position of the ball.

4 Raising your hips through the swing.

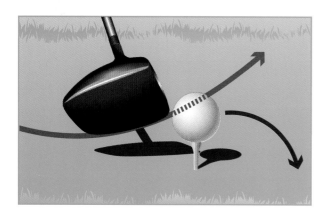

A top is when the bottom of your club makes contact with the top half of the ball, so the ball travels only a few yards from the tee.

To avoid topping the ball when you are under pressure, bear in mind this mnemonic: **Be the Big Friendly Giant (BFG).**

'B' stands for Breathe. Take 10 seconds to take good, deep breaths. Close your eyes, get the oxygen flowing through your body and tense and then relax your muscles.

'F' stands for Flex. Shake your arms and your legs to make everything feel more loose and relaxed. Ensure that there is some flex in your legs, so that they are not rigid.

'G' stands for Grip. When you get nervous and tense, you will automatically grip the club tighter. Make a conscious effort to hold the club more lightly to relieve that tension.

Golf's biggest myth is that topping is caused by lifting your head. This is not true, and is explained in more detail on page 34.

Do not be embarrassed about topping the ball. Everyone tops the ball from time to time, so shake off the shame and check out the cures for this common affliction.

➕ On-course first aid and long-term recovery

FIXES	GO TO PAGE
● Constant topping	p34
● The occasional topper	p35
● The cure for topping	p42

Hitting fat and skying

When your club catches the ground before the ball, digging into the turf before making contact, you have caught it fat – or heavy. This is another depressing fault as a lot of energy and effort goes into hitting the ball nowhere.

This problem occurs when you are too eager to get the ball airborne and forget that it should actually be swept away, using a smooth swing. In your eagerness to hit the ball you snatch at it and your swing arc dips, which means that your club approaches the ball nearer the ground than when you took the club away. The result is that you catch the turf before the ball.

Skying the ball is a very similar problem to catching it heavy, and is probably most likely to happen when you use a driver. When you sky the ball your club makes contact with the bottom of the ball, firing it skyward but not forwards, leading to a high-ballooned shot (see page 21).

These faults are caused by the same problem – you swing too steeply to the bottom of the ball and either catch the ground early or balloon the ball skyward.

Three common causes of hitting fat and skying are:

1 Trying to keep your head down.

2 Too much flex in your knees.

3 Teeing the ball too high.

Have a look at the on-course first aid for help with these difficulties.

Catching the ball heavy and skying the ball are similar problems. The club comes towards impact too steeply, either hitting the ground or the bottom of the ball.

✚ On-course first aid and long-term recovery

FIXES	GO TO PAGE
● Can't stop fatting	p32
● Fatting under pressure	p32
● End fatting forever	p42
● Can't stop skying	p33

Inconsistency and inaccuracy

Being inconsistent and inaccurate will always lead to high numbers on a card but a lot of faults can be down to something as simple as sloppy preparation or shot selection, as opposed to a fundamental swing flaw.

Playing well off the tee on a consistent basis will have a beneficial effect on your entire game. You will shave shots off your card if you can regularly hit the fairway from the tee and avoid the rough or wasting strokes with fluffed tee shots.

You can become more consistent without even practising just by using common sense. Here are the three most common mistakes made by amateurs during a round – avoid them and you'll save yourself five shots:

1 Taking a driver all the time. Don't forget your other woods, longer irons and utility clubs, which are easier to hit with and control without losing distance.

2 On par-3s, selecting a club for your best strike. Golfers are always short because they use the club that will reach with their best shot. How often do you hit your best shot per round? Always take a club that will get you there comfortably.

3 Not using the whole tee-box. Different spots on the tee will give you better angles to the green or fairway than others – think before you peg it up.

Better shot preparation can help you save five shots a round without even practicing.

On-course first aid and long-term recovery	
FIXES	**GO TO PAGE**
● Consistently inconsistent	p36
● Missing right, missing left	p37
● Lost confidence from the tee	p37
● Never miss a fairway again	p43

Lacking distance from the tee

Many of the most athletic and strong people in the world hit the ball nowhere. Many of the most slight and spindly people in the world hit the ball huge distances – take a look at rising US star Charles Howell III. He hits the ball so far because he has a good, powerful technique and amazing flexibility. He coils his body up like a spring as he takes the club back and then unwinds with incredible force. He keeps the lower half of his body as still as possible, while rotating his shoulders and the upper half of his body as far back as he can. So despite not being the strongest golfer on the planet, his flexibility makes his clubhead travel at awesome speeds, which translates into huge shots.

Power comes firstly from technique and secondly from brawn but simple changes

➕ On-course first aid and long-term recovery

FIXES	GO TO PAGE
● Always short from the tee	p30
● Weak from time to time	p31
● Skying the ball regularly	p33
● A top power tip	p43

can add length to a drive. If you are losing distance through skying the ball – if your ball balloons high into the air but only a few metres forward – your swing needs some work.

Power comes first from good technique and flexibility and then from strength.

A few simple adjustments to your swing can add metres to your driving, whatever your shape or size.

Slicing and pulling the ball

It may seem strange but a pull and a slice happen for almost identical reasons. The faults in the swing are actually the same, even though the results are vastly different. Both a pull and a slice are caused by a swing that veers outside the ball-to-target line and cuts across the ball. This means that the club strikes the ball at an angle, causing it to fly off at an angle.

With a slice, the clubhead is open or square to the target line at impact, putting sidespin on the ball and curving it right. With a pull, the clubhead is square to the swing path you have created. It is aiming straight down that out-to-in line, so you hit the ball straight left.

Quick fix

Pulls and slices, in common with most mistakes in the golf swing, originate from faults in the way you address the ball. As part of your immediate first aid for slicing or pulling the ball, use this Quick fix to check that you are addressing the ball properly.

❓ Where do you position the ball?
With a driver, fairway-wood or long-iron, the ball should be forward in your stance, opposite your left heel. The more forward it is, the more likely you are to slice the ball, so don't let it creep outside your stance.

❓ What should the grip be like?
You should have developed a solid neutral grip with two knuckles visible on your left hand at address. If you can see fewer than two, your left hand has weakened and that will open your clubface through the swing and cause a slice.

KEEP IT NEUTRAL

A neutral grip means that both your right and left hands have an equal effect on the club. If one hand controls the club more than the other, it is difficult to bring the club back square to the ball. If you have a neutral grip, you will be able to see two knuckles on your left hand at address and your right thumb will point slightly down the left of the shaft (when you look at your grip in your address position). Golfers often grip the club too tightly, which can lead to a strengthening of the right hand. Imagine you are holding a budgie when you have a club in your hands – you don't want to let it escape but you also don't want to crush it!

❓ How do you get the alignment right?
The more you slice, the further left you may try to aim as a means of compensating for hitting the ball right. The further left you aim, the more you are likely to slice the ball. The first step to redemption is simply to aim at the target. Make sure you keep your shoulders, knees, hips and toes all parallel to the ball-to-target line. Don't give in to temptation and compensate by aiming left.

❓ What is the best way to distribute your weight?
At address, your weight should be evenly distributed across your feet, maybe favouring your right foot. If you have weight on your left foot, you may send the ball out right.

Vicious, wild slicing

The vicious slice will, more often than not, be related to the manner in which you draw the club back from the ball because that determines the way you bring it back towards impact. The big slice comes when you swing outside the ball-to-target line and cut across the ball.

Quick fixes

Make like a baseball player
Carry out a few practice strokes by swinging the club as though it is a baseball bat. This will automatically put your back in a good position, will give you a feeling for a square swing path and a natural, neutral grip. When you come to hit the ball, replicate this feeling by bending from your hips to address the ball.

Keep your swing square to the ball-to-target line
To keep your swing in a good position throughout, hold the club steady when you have reached the halfway back point. Make sure the butt end of the grip points either at the ball or in-between the ball and your feet. This will keep you online through the whole swing and should calm down vicious slicing.

Hold the club out in your left hand and naturally bring your right hand on to it.

Swing the club like a baseball player would with this natural, neutral grip.

The occasional slice

When you feel under pressure, the slice may appear. If you lose rhythm and tempo you may start the downswing by over-emphasising the use of your upper body rather than your legs. This may be a permanent problem but it is one that is most likely to rear its ugly head when you feel anxious.

This fault is known as 'coming over the top'. You are nervous and need a good, solid drive. It may be the first tee or it may be the last tee – but you are feeling the heat.

Quick fixes

Three thoughts to keep your swing sweet

1 Keep your rhythm by carrying out some gentle practice swings and waggles whilst holding the club loosely.

2 Start your downswing with your hips and not your shoulders and then let the club follow through naturally.

3 Keep your right elbow close to your right hip on the downswing.

Make practice swings until you can picture in your mind a great, straight shot. Visualizing the shot before swinging can make all the difference.

The power of thought

If you are ever under pressure and feel a wild drive coming on, make some practice swings and picture in your mind the good drive that you need. Keep making practice swings until you have a crystal image in your mind's eye of that decent shot sailing down the middle of the fairway. It can make the difference between winning and losing the game.

When under pressure, have *one* key thought that you can concentrate on to prevent a slice. Practise until you find a thought that works.

Pulling left

The pull and the slice are very similar faults with wildly different results so most slice tips are applicable for a pull. In case nothing on the previous pages worked for you, try these.

Quick fixes

Square shoulders
In your set-up routine, hold the club behind the ball in your left hand only. Once you've checked the ball is not positioned too far forward, set your knees, hips, shoulders and feet square to the target; only then should you put your right hand on the club. Now check your shoulder alignment. This should naturally align you square.

A slice can become a friend if it is controlled and not too vicious. Many of the world's best golfers hit the ball so that it moves gently from left to right in its flight. This is called a fade. Colin Montgomerie won seven European Tour Order of Merits in succession by starting the ball slightly left and letting it drift into the middle of the fairway. The reason this shape is so good is that the ball will land softly with backspin so it is easy to control when it hits the green. If you hit the ball from right to left, with a draw, the ball will have more topspin and may run-out more.

Use the left-hand first set-up drill to find decent alignment and cure a pull.

Stay centred
If your hips, knees and feet are square to the ball but your shoulders are aligned left of the target, you could pull the shot. If the ball is too far forward in your stance, you may find your shoulders are drawn to the left, so keep it central.

Hooking and pushing the ball

A push and a hook are often down to the same faults in the swing. They both originate from an in-to-out swing path where the club travels from inside the target line to outside. If your clubface is square to the swing path, you will push or block the ball right; if the clubface is aiming left, you will put topspin on the ball and will hook it left.

A hook is often described as a good player's bad shot because you are using your hands well at impact. Many of the best golfers have in-to-out swing paths through the hitting area – the 2003 US Open Champion Jim Furyk is a classic example – so if this is your fault, you are doing something right! As always, checking your set-up is crucial.

Quick fixes

Addressing the ball

Hooks and pushes can be corrected by examining the way you set yourself up to hit the ball. As part of your immediate first aid for hooking or pushing the ball, use this Quick fix to check that you are addressing the ball properly.

? What might be wrong with the grip?
A strong right-handed grip – one in which you are unable to see any knuckles on the right hand when you look down at address – will close the clubface through the swing and will cause a hook.

THE PRIZED DRAW

A controlled hook, or draw, is a good tool. It can get you out of trouble by helping you weave around trees, while still gaining distance up the fairway. It is an aggressive shot-shape that travels further and with more penetration against the wind than a fade.

? Where do you position the ball?
Off the tee, the ball needs to be forward in the stance. Do not have it central or opposite the right foot.

? How do you get the alignment correct?
If you are hooking the ball, you may be inclined to aim right of the target to allow for the hook shape but this is likely to create an in-to-out swing. So you should simply aim at the target. Keep your shoulders, knees, hips and toes all parallel to the ball-to-target line and the ball is much more likely to go straight.

? What is the best way to distribute your weight?
Keep your weight evenly distributed across both feet. You need a solid platform for a solid swing, so leaving too much weight on your left side, for example, can cause all sorts of difficulties.

Vicious, wild hooking

A hook is depressing because the ball starts left of the target and just keeps going. Try these simple cures to avoid a destructive topspin hook.

Quick fixes

Smoothing your swing
If the ball is starting left and travelling further left, you are hitting a pull-hook. You are making the same mistakes as when you slice, in that you are swinging the club from out-to-in, but are rotating your hands through impact. Try the drill on page 38, the headcover drill, to keep your swing smooth. You may find you have a soft draw but this is preferable to an angry duck-hook.

Slow and steady
Avoid taking the club back too quickly on the inside. This happens when you take the clubhead away from the ball but whip the

PRACTICE TIP

In practice, stick a barrier such as an umbrella in the ground a few feet behind the clubhead when you are about to address it. Make some practice swings, avoiding the umbrella. This will force you to keep the clubhead either outside or on the ball-to-target line. If you hit the umbrella on your backswing, you have taken the club back on the inside.

clubhead behind you. Make some practice swings concentrating on keeping the clubhead in front of you throughout your swing, then replicate that feeling when you are over the ball. Here is a good swing thought: move the butt of the club first, then the clubhead.

This is a good position to be in on the first movement of your backswing and will help a straight shot.

Make sure your shaft is parallel to the ball-to-target line at this point of your backswing.

Do not let the clubhead get behind you in the swing as this may well lead to a hooked shot.

The occasional hook

An occasional hook could be down to your grip getting strong when you are under pressure. If you have concentrated on your alignment and takeaway, making sure these are square in your pre-shot set-up, but you have still hooked the ball, check your grip.

Quick fix

Grip check points:

1 A strong grip will close the clubface at impact and cause a hook.

2 You want to be able to see at least two knuckles on the back of your right hand. The fewer you see, the stronger the grip.

3 You don't want to see any more than two knuckles on your left hand. The more you see, the stronger the grip.

Grip Building: let your hands hang by your sides with your forearms slightly turned in. Bring your left hand on to the club first, then add your right hand. This is a neutral grip.

GRIP BUILDING DRILL

If you are struggling to find a decent, neutral grip, try this routine to find the cure.

1 Let your arms hang by your sides so that your palms are turned slightly inwards, towards your thighs. This is how they should look when they are placed on the club.

2 Keep your left hand by your side and then place the club in the fingers of your left hand. Keep your forearm in the same position throughout.

3 Now bring your right hand across, keeping your forearms turned in slightly, and place it on the club. This is a neutral grip.

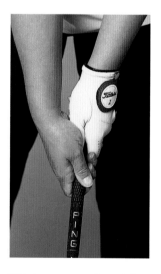

This is a strong grip and the right hand is too far underneath the club. This could well lead to a hook.

This is a good, neutral grip. This kind of grip will give the best chance of controlling the shot.

Pushing the ball right

Pushing the ball is probably the only mistake you should be happiest about making, as it is the closest to a decent strike. This is of little comfort, though, when you are continually dropping the ball out of a bush after pushing it into the rough.

Poor alignment tends to be the reason for pushing the ball, so the best solution is to build a set-up routine that keeps you square to the target. A push will come when your hips, knees and feet are square but your shoulders aim right.

Quick fix

The comfort zone
Add this drill to your pre-shot routine to help cure pushed shots.

HOW GOLFERS CAN GROW TO LOVE A HOOK

There are occasions when you will want to shape the ball in the air from right to left as the draw has a number of attractive properties. Not only can you manufacture shots around obstacles such as trees and bunkers, but a draw has a more piercing flight and roll. The topspin on the ball will add distance to the shot and will drive the ball further through a head wind. For this reason, many top golfers, including Bernhard Langer, regularly hit the ball with a soft draw. It helps negate the effects of the elements and produces great consistency.

With your right hand hold the club behind the ball. This encourages you to align your shoulders more left than before.

Next, place your feet, knees and hips in position, parallel to the target line, while keeping the clubface square.

Finally, place your left hand on the club. It should now feel uncomfortable to align your shoulders right of the target.

Hitting short off the tee

From time to time, you'll look at a fellow golfer (or even yourself) and think they should hit the ball huge distances but they don't. Many golfers do not utilize their fundamental power because of simple technical faults. Overswinging is the most common cause of weak golf as you lose the elastic power of a tightly controlled backswing. Power is also lost when your wrists are not hinged properly.

Quick fixes

Dealing with the overswing
The key is to have your left arm straightened at the top, so there is space between your right shoulder and hands. Make sure you hinge your wrists or you'll still lose power.

Hinging the wrists
Follow these three steps to practise hinging your wrists:

1 Hold the bottom of the grip in the first two fingers of your right hand and the top with the first two of your left.

2 Swing the club back to halfway so your wrists naturally sit at 90 degrees to your forearms.

3 Swing through and hold at 90 degrees in the finish.

This gives a feel for the correct positions through the swing and develops a decent wrist hinge naturally. It is a great way to warm up.

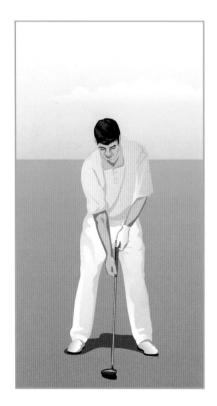

Hold the club with two fingers only at either end of the grip.

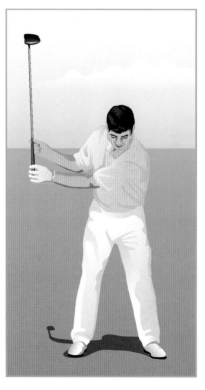

Make a backswing and allow the weight to hinge your wrists at right-angles.

Now swing through letting your wrists re-hinge.

Weak from time to time

Occasional weakness comes from tension. You really want to hit a big drive so you try hard to smash it. The result is that you tense up and all your muscles contract and become firm, like a piece of wood, instead of loose and flexible, like an elastic band.

Quick fix

Three tips to release the on-course tension that leads to weak shots:

1 Add a waggle. Waggling the club before hitting tee-shots loosens the muscles and regains the suppleness lost through tension. Also, try not grounding the club before making a backswing as this will help keep the flow in your swing.

2 Take a deep breath. Hold a deep breath for a few seconds, then exhale long and deep. Do this twice before hitting. Move your hands up to your chest as you breathe in, then let them drop as you exhale.

3 Take your left, little finger off the club. Then make some practice swings. This allows the clubhead to swing more freely and naturally. Keep repeating these swings until you feel more supple and less tense.

THE DISTANCE MYTH

There is a school of thought that suggests teeing the ball low will gain extra distance. In fact, teeing the ball low may be a reason for your lack of distance. Modern equipment, both balls and clubs, are designed to make your ball fly high and far – that low, penetrating strike is so last century! If you watch any professional event live, you will see that players' ball flights are, generally, high and far, not low and piercing. You may not see this so clearly if you are watching on television. Of course, Tour professionals have the skill to hit a low one if needed but a good rule is: 'Tee it high – let it fly'.

Horror shots

If you find you are fatting the ball consistently from the tee, you are probably suffering from some sloppy address faults, which can easily be altered. The main reason for fatting the ball is your swing arc dipping, which means you will approach the ball nearer the ground than when you took the club away. You may also find that if you are fatting the ball when under pressure, tension in your muscles might be causing a loss of momentum.

Quick fixes

Address checklist:

? Are you too close to the ball?
If you stand too close, you are liable to pick the club up steeply and could well catch turf before the ball. You may also hit the bottom of the ball, leading to a skied shot.

? Is the ball back in your stance?
Again, this may encourage you to pick the club up too sharply, hit down on it too steeply and catch the turf.

? Is your chin on your chest at address?
If it is, you will struggle to turn your shoulders and you will end up hitting at the ball with your hands and arms as opposed to a sweeping swing.

Too much tension
If you are tense over the ball, all your muscles will contract and be stiff, giving you less control over the swing. To avoid this all-over-body tension, channel it into one useful area. Squeeze firmly with the last three fingers of your top hand. This forces all that tension into one place and shortens your swing arc, making you more likely to catch the ball thin than fat.

Focus all your tension into the last three fingers of your top hand. Squeeze the club tightly with these fingers.

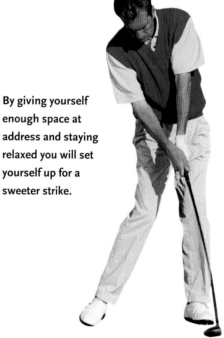

By giving yourself enough space at address and staying relaxed you will set yourself up for a sweeter strike.

Height but no distance

If you have fired the ball from the tee high into the air, but not managed any significant distance forward, you have 'skied' the ball. Skying is a common mistake and it happens when your driver catches the bottom half of the ball. A skied drive usually means you have had a steep downswing and the clubhead has chopped under the ball.

Quick fixes

Winning width
Concentrate on brushing the bottom of the club along the grass for at least a foot as you take the club back. This will give your swing width and stop it being too steep. It will also help your weight shift correctly on to your right side.

Colin Montgomerie, seven times European Tour Order of Merit winner, has one simple thought whenever he tees up: 'Low and slow'.

The right height
Skying the ball may come down to one simple problem – you have teed the ball up too high. This is an easy mistake to make, especially in the modern age where you have drivers with big, bulky clubheads. Tee the ball up so that half of it is above the top of the club. Any higher and you could sky it.

If it is good enough for Monty, it is good enough for you. As you take the club away keep it low and slow.

With modern-day clubs and balls it is crucial to tee the ball at the right height .

Constant topping

Topping happens when a golfer has a decent address position, with well-flexed legs, but then straightens them on the backswing. The club returns to a higher position than when it left, producing a top. As the ball travels no distance, it looks like an embarrassing mistake.

The top is caused by straightening your legs on the backswing – not by lifting your head, as is commonly thought.

Quick fixes

Tee time

A simple on-course recovery aid avoids any technical thoughts and concentrates on feel. If you have hit a few tops in a row, put a tee-peg in the ground and make some practice swings just trying to clip the top of the tee peg. Have one thought as you swing: 'Take the tee.' Concentrate on taking that tee out of the ground and nothing else. Then return to the ball with that swing feel tuned into your address position.

Forward thinking

One simple cause of the topped shot is ball position. Make sure the ball is not too far back in your stance as this will force you to hit too early in your swing. By placing the ball further forward in your stance, you will catch it in the sweeping upwards part of your swing, which helps you launch the ball high into the air, gaining extra distance from a decent strike.

THE BIGGEST GOLF MYTH

The biggest mistake that golfers make, especially after topping the ball, is to think: 'Keep my head down.' This is appallingly wrong and anyone who tells you this is badly misguided. This mistake comes from the straightening of the legs or collapsing of the left arm, not from lifting your head. Your head has to move slightly in the golf swing. Otherwise, you will not be able to turn your shoulders properly, for one thing. There are also a number of other dreadful faults caused by this mythical piece of 'good advice' – the biggest myth in golf.

Place the ball forward in your stance and catch it on the sweeping upward section of your swing.

Occasional topping

All topped shots originate from one fault: failing to keep, throughout your swing, the same height you established when addressing the ball. So when you are tense or feeling under pressure, you may lose some rhythm in your swing and lift in your backswing. This causes a top at impact.

Quick fixes

Hips and back

As soon as you feel under pressure and know you've topped the ball in the past in a similar situation, you need a solid swing reminder. Try these two positive thoughts to avoid a topped shot: 'Keep hips level throughout my swing'; 'Swing around my back.' Imagine your back as a hinge that you rotate around but cannot move up and down. By keeping your hips level, this will be easy and will lead to an improved and more consistent strike – cutting out topped shots.

HOW TO USE THESE TIPS

To use these occasional tips to best advantage, you must establish which fault applies to you and then keep that one key thought for those pressure shots. If you muddle your thinking with more than one piece of advice, they will not only seem conflicting, but also confusing.

Straight left

A top can arise from the left arm collapsing into a 'chicken wing' position and pulling the club up from the ball. This can happen when you are anxious to see where the ball has gone and lose your rhythm. Remember: 'Left arm straight through downswing.' This should keep your driver sweeping through the ball, avoiding a top.

Give yourself enough room at address.

Think: 'Swing around my back' through the backswing.

Think: 'Keep the hips level through the swing.'

Keep the left arm straight through the downswing.

Inconsistency and inaccuracy

Inconsistency off the tee often comes down to poor preparation for the shot. Poor drives will probably appear when you least need them: when you are facing a tricky drive or a pressurized situation.

You need to sort out a good pre-shot routine: a consistent routine leads to consistent driving. It does not have to be complicated and it should certainly not take long, but a consistent pre-shot routine will cut out most of those embarrassing 'twice-a-round' fluffed drives.

A good routine is a comfort zone that you can fall back into when you feel the heat. It makes everything seem natural and easy. Without a good routine you might say to yourself: 'How do I hit this drive?' With a good routine, you are more likely to say: 'Where do I hit it?' It will put you in a much more positive frame of mind.

Quick fix

Four keys to a good routine

1 Pick a target in the distance and 'see' your shot, in your mind's eye.

2 Have two practice swings from behind the ball to loosen up and 'feel' the shot.

3 Take a square address position and waggle the club until you are comfortable.

4 Swing within two seconds of feeling comfortable. If you wait five seconds before taking the club back, all you will have gleaned from your preparation will be lost. It will mean nothing in your swing. You must keep the process of hitting the ball flowing and make sure your routine is short and smooth.

Pick a target.   **Have two practice swings.**   **Take a square address.**   **Swing within two seconds.**

Missing right and missing left

If there is inconsistency in your driving, you may still be doing most things properly. Your swing and basic technique may be solid but your alignment and shot selection may be awry. Inconsistency off the tee may also be due to loss of confidence. There are times when you should simply let your driver gather dust for a round if you've lost the confidence to use it and go for a smaller, more controllable club.

Quick fixes

Reduce your target

If you are missing left and right from the tee, you could be picking too big a target. When selecting a line, don't simply aim at the big tree behind the green, or the large fairway bunker, pick a more specific point. Select the corner of the bunker, or a branch of the tree. This will focus aim accurately and if you miss left or right, you will be left or right of a small point and more likely to be on the fairway.

A simple test

Check your alignment if you are missing fairways left and right. When waiting to play, pick a target, place a club along your toes and take up your address position. Stand back and see where the club is pointing.

Decent alignment is the key to hitting straight, consistent golf shots. Never stop checking in practice.

If it is aimed straight at the target, you will be aligned too far right because your feet, shoulders, knees and hips need to be parallel to the ball-to-target line, not on it.

Reduce power

A fairway wood or a mid-iron from the tee may lose you 18m (20yd), but isn't that a fair sacrifice for playing your next shot from the fairway?

When your confidence goes, in terms of hitting with your driver, and that happens to everyone from time to time, clever golf is to concentrate on keeping the ball in play by using a club with which you are more comfortable. This will, in turn, boost your confidence and you'll be more likely to use the driver later in the round.

Don't be too proud to return a driver to your bag and instead take an iron off the tee.

The cure for slicing and pulling

Over the years, there have been numerous cures, fixes and drills for mending the slice, some fantastical and weird, some simple and effective. Outlined below are two of the most effective tips and drills you can work on to rid yourself of your slice for good.

Quick fix

Get your address right
Most problems do start with the address position. The crucial elements for a good address to avoid the slice are:
• Spine angle
• Alignment

Good spine angle
Your spine should be angled about ten degrees away from the target at address, putting the weight on your right foot slightly more than your left. From this position, it will be easier to swing to the top of the backswing on plane.

QUICK SLICE CURE DRILL

When you are waiting for your tee-shot, go through some practice swings with a clubhead cover tucked under your right armpit. Concentrate on keeping the cover there through the entire swing – this will stop you coming over the top. Replicate that feeling when you are over the ball.

If you are having difficulty developing this angle because it feels totally unnatural, try carrying out some practice swings on a slope so that your left foot is higher than your right. This will automatically put you in the right position at address as the slope will angle you away from the target. Then replicate that feeling when you are over the ball.

Take an address position on an up-slope with your front (left) foot higher than your back (right) foot. Then make some practice swings. This drill will automatically give you a decent spine angle.

Maintaining good alignment

This is perhaps the most crucial element to the swing and the one that causes the most problems without you realizing their root cause. Any time you are on the range, you should use this simple practice technique to drill decent alignment into your game.

Whenever you are working on your game, lay some clubs down so you can drill good alignment.

At the top of your backswing, check that the grooves on your clubface are square to the target.

Quick fixes

Drilling good alignment

1 Place two clubs on the ground parallel to each other. Run one along your toes and the other on the far side of the ball. Keep the ball in the middle of these shafts.

2 Now align yourself square to the shafts, which should be parallel to the target line.

3 Hit every practice shot from this position, always making sure you are square to the clubs.

Angles, angles, angles

If you have a neutral grip, the angle of the clubface at the top of your backswing could affect your strike. If it is open, you may push or slice the ball. When practising, try this angle-check drill:

1 Place a mirror in front of you and set up your address so that your toes are pointing at the mirror.

2 Swing to the top of your backswing and hold that position.

3 Look at the grooves on the club. Which way are they pointing?

4 If the grooves on the club point to the sky, you have a closed clubface.

5 If the toe of the club points to the ground, it is open.

6 If the grooves are at a 45 degree angle to the ground you are square.

7 Practise a square position at the top of your swing so that you avoid the slice and pull.

The cure for hooking and pushing

These faults are the best faults you can suffer. It means there is a lot to work with in your swing and that you have an instinctive, powerful hand action through the ball. The push is very close to a high-quality strike. So try these practice drills to straighten that push and turn a hook into a controlled draw.

Quick fixes

Sort out your takeaway
If you take the club inside the line on the takeaway, you will struggle to avoid a hook. If this is causing the trouble, try this practice drill: first, place two clubs along the line of your feet end to end, so they stretch behind you. Then take an address position over the ball.

Take the club away from the ball and hold it at waist height and check your position. If the club is crossing the line of the clubs on the ground, you are taking it inside – it should instead be directly online with these clubs. Once you are on-line, swing to the top and strike the ball. Hit a bucket of balls holding the on-line position halfway before swinging to the top and striking.

Obstacle drill
This is designed to stop you taking the club on the inside by placing an object such as a headcover inside the line on your initial takeaway. If you hit this headcover either on the way back or on the downswing, you will be swinging from in-to-out and may hook or push the ball.

Try to keep your club parallel to the clubs on the ground at the halfway back position.

The obstacle drill forces you to not come from the inside, which may lead to a hook.

Staying in line

Pushing is often down to poor alignment. Another common cause is the ball position – make sure the ball is not too far back at address as this can cause a hook. The alignment drill you should use to cure a push is exactly the same as that for a pull.

Quick fixes

Alignment, alignment, alignment

1 Place two clubs on the ground parallel to each other.

2 Align yourself square to the shafts, which are parallel to the target line.

3 Hit every practice shot from this position, making sure you are square to the clubs.

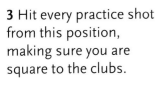

It is good to keep a check on your alignment even if you are playing well. You will see the best players in the world doing this drill at any professional event.

Stand away

Have a practice session hitting balls with your left toe in line with your right heel – giving you a very open stance. This forces you to hit from outside the line and gives you room to swing the club left after impact. When you have hit a number of shots, recreate that swing from a normal address position.

'WHY DO I HOOK AND SLICE MY LONG CLUBS AND NOT MY SHORT?'

A slice and a hook come from sidespin. The more sidespin, the greater the hook or slice. When a steep-faced driver hits a ball, there is little backspin because there is little loft on the club and without backspin there is nothing to negate the sidespin. When you play a 9-iron, there is much more loft, so you will have more backspin, and the sidespin has less effect.

This is a fantastic drill for straightening your hook. The very open stance will make it nearly impossible to hook the ball.

Avoid the fat and skied shot

Here is a decent practice drill that will make a shallow swing second nature, ridding you of the fat and skied drive forever. Both problems are the result of a steep downswing.

Quick fixes

The push-ball drill

1 When you are driving on the range, place a second ball 25cm (10in) behind the ball you are striking.

2 As you start your backswing, gently push it away. This will help you obtain a flatter, sweeping swing, making you start smoothly.

Long-term thought
A fat or sky is also down to a loss of rhythm, where the golfer takes the club away sharply with hands and arms instead of a smooth, one piece takeaway. Bear in mind, as you should for all your shots, Tony Jacklin's one swing thought that he has used throughout a lengthy and successful career: 'Wide and smooth.'

Topping cure
To avoid topping the ball, keep a good posture throughout practice with these ideas:

1 Concentrate on the back of the ball.

2 On sunny days, set up so you can see if your shadow is moving up as you swing back.

3 Use your reflection in a window or mirror to check the same.

You want to keep the same spine angle throughout, as any movement could lead to a top.

To avoid topped shots, practise taking the club away low to the ground.

'Wide and smooth' or 'slow and low' – it is simple to stop topping forever.

A great tool for drilling decent posture, to improve your game, is a mirror.

Increase your power forever

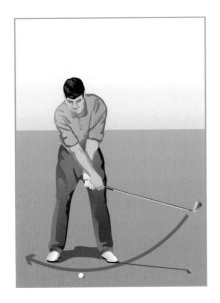

Start the swing with your wrists 'released' and beyond the ball.

Swing halfway back, letting the weight of the club hinge your wrists.

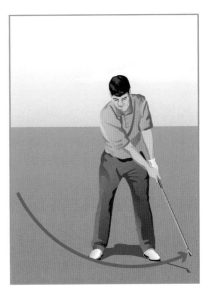

Now swing through to impact and see what a difference in power is made.

Increasing power is more about better technique than extra brawn. Improving the timing of your swing will gain you vital distance off the tee.

Quick fixes

Use this drill on the range to increase your power

1 Think of the takeaway as a 'swing-away', to stop you making a slow jerky first move in the swing.

2 Start your swing-away with the club a couple of feet in front of the ball, then swing back. This creates good timing and swing plane, as well as increasing the momentum of the strike.

A similar drill is to start beyond the ball again, but with your wrists released already. Swing the club back over the ball, letting the wrists hinge halfway back and then hit the ball. You will feel

increased leverage – use of wrists and forearms – in your swing, which means increased power.

Keep driving consistently

To stay on the fairway, keep a continual check on your posture, address position and alignment. These basics affect your consistency from the tee.

Posture control

A way to obtain good posture is to stand upright and hold a club across the top of your thighs. Then gently push the club into your body and tilt forwards while keeping your spine nice and straight.

Ball position

1 Keep a continual check on this and don't let the ball go too far back in your stance.

2 The longer the club, the more forward the ball position should be.

FROM THE FAIRWAY

One of the most common mistakes made from the fairway is the thinned shot, particularly with long irons. This is where the clubhead makes contact with the top half of the ball and, as a result, the ball fails to fly very far in the air.

You can often get away with a thinned iron shot, as the ball may well run a similar distance to what you intended, but the closer to the green you are the less desirable the shot. It can also really hurt your hands, especially on a cold day.

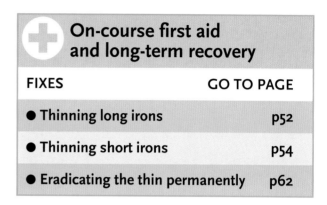

Thinning shots

✚ On-course first aid and long-term recovery

FIXES	GO TO PAGE
● Thinning long irons	p52
● Thinning short irons	p54
● Eradicating the thin permanently	p62

Solid posture at address is the key for good contact with any iron shot.

Avoiding a thinned shot is down to a solid position at the top.

Hitting fat shots

Taking big divots can be a good thing: how often do you see Phil Mickelson exploding a ball from the fairway without a huge, earthy gouge? But take the divot in the wrong place and you are left with that depressing fat shot, where you've caught too much ground and not enough ball.

This is a problem that is more likely to strike with your irons than with your fairway woods. The fairway woods will bounce off the top of the turf, whereas an iron, with its sharper leading edge, will dig in, diverting the energy you have put into the shot into the ground and not into the ball.

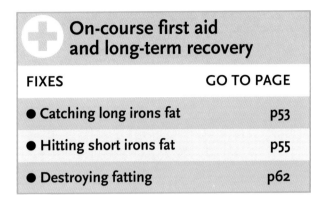

On-course first aid and long-term recovery

FIXES	GO TO PAGE
● Catching long irons fat	p53
● Hitting short irons fat	p55
● Destroying fatting	p62

Catching the ball fat is more likely to happen with iron shots than fairway woods.

A large divot from the wrong place can lead to weak and problematic iron shots.

Ball disappears straight right

You are not supposed to mention it – just as actors are not supposed to use the word 'Macbeth' backstage, so golfers avoid using the term 'shank' – because it is one of the most surprising and painful errors in golf. You'll be swinging well and having a good round and then, all of a sudden, a shank bites you and you walk away with an eight.

Shanks are contagious. Once you have had one, your next shot feels impossible and is often a shank as well. You will shank a short iron more often than a driver or fairway wood but before you throw your clubs in the lake, try these on-course cures.

It happens to the best of them

You are in good company if you shank. Professionals often describe the shank as a shot that is nearly perfect – technically you have not done that much wrong. So it is no surprise that a shank can attack even the best golfers as Darren Clarke discovered in the final round of the Open Championship at Royal Troon in 1997. High on the leaderboard, he shanked a tee-shot early on in his round to drop two shots and ultimately finish second.

There is no more depressing feeling than a shank – the ball disappears at almost right angles into the angriest-looking bush, and you have no idea where the shot has come from as your swing felt fine. You may feel (and look) stupid, but do not despair – turn to the On-course cures for advice.

✚ On-course first aid and long-term recovery

FIXES	GO TO PAGE
● The occasional shank	p56
● Regular shanking	p56
● Destroying the shank	p64

Bad lies and muddy balls

Finding your ball in a divot in the middle of the fairway can often seem like a disaster. It is only a mini-crisis, in fact, and a few set-up changes can help you escape the nastiest of unfair lies. Another hazard, usually encountered on rain-drenched courses, is a clump of mud becoming stuck to the side of your ball. You may not be too thrilled to see this but you have to deal with it.

'The more I practise, the luckier I get.' So said the great South African golfer Gary Player – and he is still saying it today. There is one thing you need when playing from tough situations, and that is luck. The best way to generate that luck – if such a thing is possible – is to regularly practise hitting from those killer lies. Find some thick rough at the edge of the practice range and blast a dozen balls from it. Place balls in divots and on bare ground to see how they react on different surfaces. You will discover

➕ On-course first aid and long-term recovery	
FIXES	**GO TO PAGE**
● **Stuck in divots**	P57
● **Playing a muddied ball**	P57
● **Troublesome lies**	P57

consistency and develop greater confidence through practising from problem spots.

In his University days, Tiger Woods was spotted alone on the range in a howling gale and horizontal rain. 'What the hell are you doing?' yelled a friend. 'Practising for the British Open,' the future World number one replied.

REPAIRING TROUBLE

Just because you feel hard-done-by when you find yourself in a divot, there is no need to take revenge on the rest of the golfing world by leaving holes all over the fairways. It is an important part of golf etiquette to replace divots from the fairway at all times – so make sure you do it! It is in the interests of all golfers to look after each element of the course, so always repair your pitch marks on the greens and rake the bunkers.

Hitting from a hillside lie

The joys of the golf course are the perfectly manicured greens and rolling, undulating fairways set against a magnificent backdrop. You soon forget all about that view when you end up on one of those undulations, with the ball either above or below your feet.

It is not easy to play off the side of a hill but such shots can be mastered. Don't curse your bad luck; instead, keep your head and find the putting surface. There are a few simple rules that can help you conquer the severest of slopes.

On-course first aid and long-term recovery

FIXES	GO TO PAGE
● Hitting the ball to the right when ball is below feet	p58
● Hitting the ball to the left when ball is above feet	p58
● The cure for topping	p42

When the ball is above your feet, it is easy to hit it off line.

Hitting a ball from below your feet can be one of the toughest shots in the game.

Loss of distance on sloping lies

Playing a ball on a downhill lie can be awkward and losing control is easy. Similarly, playing from an uphill lie can have the strangest consequences for your ball: ballooning it upwards but not forwards.

Uphill and downhill lies can cause problems if they are not addressed correctly and with caution. Taking simple measures to avoid disastrous results will save you a lot of headaches during a round.

On-course first aid and long-term recovery

FIXES	GO TO PAGE
● Loss of distance from uphill lies	p59
● No control on a downhill slope	p59
● Sloping checks	p63

Controlling distance is the key to playing from upslopes. Always use the right club.

Swinging positively and aggressively can help overcome the tricks of a downslope.

Inaccuracy from the fairway

You've hit a drive 250m (273yd), splitting the fairway, and you are faced with a 125m (137yd) short-iron to a flat green. In your mind, you have already nailed it to 3m (9ft) and either sunk the putt or helped yourself to a solid par.

Then you find the greenside bunker, hack it out, and, distressed, you three-putt and walk off with a six. That is why this game is so cruel. Your drive didn't deserve a double-bogey but your inaccurate approach play did.

✚ On-course first aid and long-term recovery

FIXES	GO TO PAGE
● Missing the green from close range	p61
● Missing from long range	p61
● Building long-term consistency	p65

Hitting greens in regulation is crucial if you want to shoot low scores.

GREENS IN REGULATION

It can be argued that your approach play is one of the most important elements of the game. If you look at the Greens in Regulation statistics on the US Tour for the 2002 season next to the putts per round, they are revealing. (Hitting a green in regulation means that on a par-4 the golfer reached the green in two shots or less, on a par-5 in three shots or less and on a par-3 in one shot or less.)

	Money list position	GIR % (pos)	PpR % (pos)
Tiger Woods	1st	74 (1st)	29.4 (163rd)
Vijay Singh	3rd	70.7 (7th)	29.0 (106th)
Chris Riley	23rd	61.5 (176th)	27.9 (2nd)

Tiger Woods did not have the best season with the putter, but hit huge amounts of greens. He finished first on the money list. Chris Riley putted well, but did not find enough greens to make it count.

Inconsistent approach play

Many golfers find that from 150m (164yd) out, they can be deadly – occasionally. The problem is, it can be very occasional. Inconsistency from this range is the root of many high handicaps.

If you are finding that there is not enough difference in yardage between your clubs, or you are lacking the power to heave a long iron or fairway wood 200m (219yd), then there could be some technical problems and you will need to work on these.

Working out your own specific yardages is very important in developing accuracy and consistency in your game. Creating a healthy difference between each club is also vital in adding control to your game. Don't fall into

the machismo trap of trying to hit your 7-iron further than your friends. Instead, develop your own honest yardages and you will find your play will improve.

<table>
<tr><td colspan="2">➕ On-course first aid and long-term recovery</td></tr>
<tr><td>FIXES</td><td>GO TO PAGE</td></tr>
<tr><td>● Not enough power</td><td>p60</td></tr>
<tr><td>● Lack of yardage between clubs</td><td>p60</td></tr>
<tr><td>● Always leaving the ball short</td><td>p61</td></tr>
<tr><td>● Finding your hidden consistency</td><td>p65</td></tr>
</table>

Whatever your age, saving shots comes from consistency with your iron shots.

Knowing your personal yardages will breathe life into your game.

You will always have more control with a full swing than with a half-shot.

Thinning long irons

A long iron is probably the hardest club in the bag to hit. They are unforgiving when you thin the ball with them, especially on a cold winter's day, when the club will judder in your hands. You should still persevere with your long irons because there is no feeling in golf quite as good as nailing a long iron close.

Quick fixes

The long and short of it

Long irons are often thought by golfers to be bogey clubs. This is not the best mindset to have to conquer them. If you have thinned a few in a row, approach your long-iron shots in the same way as you approach your short-iron shots. The key is to use exactly the same swing – don't change anything. You will have to stand slightly further away from the ball to allow for the longer shaft but if this is uncomfortable, choke down the grip slightly, stand a touch nearer and then use your normal swing.

If you are having trouble with your long irons, think 'wedge-swing' and be confident.

Relax your grip

The main cause of a thin is a tight grip. This happens when they are faced with a tough shot into a well-guarded green or feel under pressure. When you grip tightly, you shorten your swing arc, which means that the club comes through above the ball and you thin it.

GIVE TENSION THE ELBOW

A good thought to rid yourself of tension in your arms and hands is to relax your elbows and keep them away from your body at address. From this position, it is very hard to squeeze tightly – Seve Ballesteros was a master of this technique.

Fatting the long irons

If you thin a long iron, you'll probably make some distance down the middle. If you fat one, the ball will go nowhere and you could be playing the same club again.

Quick fixes

Keep your distance
Are you standing too close to the ball? As with all regular faults, the first place you should look for answers is at address. If you are too close, you will take the club up sharply and bring it back to the ball steeply. That means you will be more likely to dig into the turf when what you really want is a shallow, sweeping swing.

On-course check
Stand with your hands dangling freely from your shoulders. Then take hold of the club and address the ball. You must keep that distance between your hands and your thighs – about a hand's width. If there is less than this, you are too close.

JUST DON'T BOTHER

The best way to avoid thinning or fatting long irons is not to use them. Most of the world's best players no longer carry 1- or 2-irons but opt for fairway woods or hybrid clubs (half wood, half iron). Many golfers find fairway woods much simpler to hit and more forgiving than long irons. There are woods of a variety of different lofts, from 3-woods up to 7- and 9-woods, the equivalent of 5- or 6-irons.

If you have fatted a few shots in a row, check you are not standing too close to the ball with your long irons.

You should have a hand's width between your thighs and grip. If there is less space than this, then you are standing too close to the ball.

Thinning short irons

If you have a wedge in your hands, you must be close to the green. If you've thinned it, you're probably through the back in trouble. It's not a nice situation to be in but don't panic. Thinning a short iron comes from a deceleration in the swing. One of the most common reasons is that you feel under pressure on the shot; the other is that you are in between clubs.

Quick fixes

Beat the pressure
When you feel under pressure, the muscles in your arms will tighten. That will shorten your swing and lose you rhythm. Add an extra practice swing to your routine, grip the club softly and keep your rhythm.

Iron out the problem
You may find yourself stuck between clubs and questioning whether to use a soft 8-iron or a hard 9-iron. This is where you must know your own game. Are you a quick swinger or a smooth rhythmical golfer? Neither is better, but we are all more one than the other. Think which you are and choose the club accordingly. If you make aggressive swings at the ball, you will be more confident hitting a 9-iron. If you are a smoother swinger, hit the 8. You should now be confident with the club in your hands, so swing full and long and do not hesitate.

Don't fall into the classic amateur trap of selecting the club suitable for your best shot. High handicap golfers hit their best shot twice a round at most – so if you find yourself saying 'I can get there with a 9 if I really nail it', take an 8 instead.

Stay relaxed and keep your breathing calm and controlled to avoid letting the pressure get to you. If you are tense you are more likely to thin a short iron through the back.

Hitting short irons fat

It has been said that missing the green with a wedge is like missing your face with a fork: you are in the scoring zone, you have no distance to the pin and you catch a short iron heavy, dropping the ball into a greenside bunker. It happens to everyone. You will catch the ball fat when you forget about the swing and start hitting at the ball. From this short distance especially, you must make your club do the work. The ball is incidental to the swing because the loft of the clubface lifts it into the air. You do not have to help it.

Quick fixes

The right feeling
To avoid hitting at the ball, try this quick practice swing to remind yourself of the correct swing feeling:

1 Put the top of the grip into your ribcage and grip down the shaft.

2 Swing backwards and forwards.

3 Move your body and arms together.

This will stop you simply hitting at the ball with your hands, and will encourage the connection between hands and body that's lost when you hit it heavy.

Add an extra wedge
By adding an extra wedge to your bag, instead of a long iron, you will have a better chance to swing positively. With more loft in your bag, you will be able to make a full, positive swing from closer in.

Take practice swings with the club pressed gently into your ribcage to enable you to find the right connection between your arms and body.

Shanking

The shank happens when the ball shoots off the hosel of the club (the lowest part of the shaft) at almost right angles to the ball-to-target line. It is a frightening fault as it often appears when you least expect it, but on-course remedies are not far away.

Quick fixes

Room to move
Simply standing too close to the ball often causes the shank. If you have just suffered from a shank, check where your hands are in relation to your thighs. You want at least a hand's width between hands and thighs so readjust your set-up to give your swing some room.

A smooth plane
A shank happens when you swing from out-to-in, throwing the clubhead away from your body as you swing down. Use this test to check your swing plane:

1 Begin your address with your back against a tree or wall.

2 Swing to the top of your backswing.

3 If you hit the obstacle behind you, you are too flat and may shank.

4 If you miss the obstacle, your swing is on plane and you will be fine.

A new routine
This may seem like a contradiction, but to avoid hitting the ball from the hosel of the club, address the ball from the hosel. This will encourage you to take the club away on-line. If you address the ball off the toe of the club, which feels like a natural cure, you may swing outside the line and cause trouble for yourself.

Make some practice swings with your back next to a wall or tree. If you find the club is hitting the obstacle behind you, then you may be in danger of shanking.

Tough lies and tough luck

Finding your ball sitting in a divot after you've sent a nice drive down the middle is not pleasant. It is also not that bad. Make a few changes and you'll never be annoyed again. Annoyingly but often inevitably, you may also find that dollops of mud attach themselves to your ball. It is best to concentrate on getting the ball on to the green as quickly as possible so you can mark it and give it a good clean.

Quick fixes

Divot solution

Playing from a divot is more about adjusting your address position than anything else – your swing will naturally alter due to the set-up changes noted below.

1 Put the ball back in your stance.

2 Play with your hands forward.

A TIP FOR TROUBLE SHOTS

A good tip for all trouble shots is to play the ball back in your stance as this will help you dig yourself out of trouble. Remember it like this: 'Right foot for Rubbish!'

3 Use a more lofted club than for a decent lie.

4 Aim slightly left as a shot from a divot can put left-to-right spin on the ball.

Be aggressive

Swing normally but be positive and aggressive. Try and take a divot out of the divot because you want to dig down to the bottom of the ball. Don't worry about your follow-through – just dig the ball out.

Mudball pointers

1 Take an extra club for the distance.

2 Play the ball back in your stance to help an aggressive strike.

3 Swing hard at the ball. Do not hold back.

Place the ball back in your stance with your hands forward.

Set-up changes will lead to a steeper backswing.

Make an aggressive downswing to the back of the ball.

Hitting accurately from a slope

Playing from a sloping lie, whether the ball is above your feet or below it, is always awkward. Sending the ball far too much to the right when it is below you is common as is hitting it left when the ball is above your feet. It is difficult and uncomfortable for any golfer to hit the ball accurately from a slope but a little bit of extra preparation can balance out the situation.

Quick fixes

Changing set-up to hit a ball below your feet

1 Use an extra club.

2 Aim left of the target as the slope will make the ball fade from left to right.

3 Hold the club at the top of your grip to aid your posture.

4 It is vitally important that you flex your knees to help you get down to the ball in as normal a position as possible.

5 Widen your stance to feel comfortable.

Changing set-up to hit a ball above your feet

1 Use less club.

2 Aim right of the target as this shot will put drawspin on the ball, making it move from right to left and travel further.

3 It is vitally important that you hinge from the waist, and this should be easier once you have choked down the grip.

4 Keep your knees flexed.

When the ball is below your feet, aim left of the target and use more club than you would for a flat lie.

The ball will hook when it is hit from above your feet. Choke down the grip and aim right of the target to allow for this.

Distance control from downhill lies

A downhill lie is a difficult place from which to conjure up a clean strike and it is easy to make some fundamental mistakes. Avoid fighting the slope and use it instead. Uphill lies can cause you difficulty in judging distance, particularly if you are set up against the slope because this may make you dig into it. Concentrate on the fundamentals of the shot and the hill will not be too large an obstacle.

Quick fixes

Hitting downhill

The key to this shot is having your shoulders parallel with the slope. On a downhill lie you will have a higher right shoulder than normal. So you want to get your weight on your lower leg. Distance control is difficult. The loft of the club will be flattened by the slope, so take less club than you'd normally need for this distance. With longer clubs you may well hit a fade, so aim slightly left of the target. Allow your weight to be released fully down the hill and through the ball, even if it means you lose balance after impact.

Getting good length from an uphill lie

Have your shoulders parallel to the slope and not set against it. Place your weight on your lower leg. This will add loft to your shot so take an extra club to compensate. Aim a little right of the target as an uphill lie will put a touch of right-to-left spin on the ball. Swing along the slope, taking the club back low and smoothly, and swing up the hill through impact. Retain your balance by transferring your weight on to your left side. Don't get stuck on your right.

Downhill lies are not only difficult to control but are hard to hit well.

Swing positively, otherwise you will thin your shot.

Do not worry about your finish position with this shot.

The reverse pivot

If you are lacking accuracy with your long
irons and finding there is no difference in
yardage between clubs, it will be because of
one of the most common technical faults in
the golf swing: the reverse pivot. If you are
missing with your long irons because they are
off-line or weak, or if there seems to be little
difference in length between your long,
middle and shorter irons, then you could be
suffering from a reverse pivot.

The reverse pivot is an incorrect shift of weight
through the swing. Instead of your weight
moving on to your right side as you take the
club away, it moves on to your left. On the
downswing, your weight then transfers
on to the right side of your body and
you finish on your back foot. You
have not used your bodyweight
through impact, so this is a weak
shot. All your irons will travel similar
distances, as you use your hands to
hit the ball and not your body.

Quick fix

Make it routine

1 Make some practice swings and,
as you take the club back, take your
left foot off the ground, forcing all
the weight on to your right. Keep
swinging until the feeling is natural.

2 When you are over the ball, think
'70–30'. This means you should have
70 per cent of your weight on your
right side at the top of the backswing
and only 30 per cent on your left.

3 Keep your right knee flexed
throughout. Do not let it straighten.

NOT ALL BAD

A reverse pivot will make long irons and
fairway woods hard to play, but you can get
away with it on shorter irons where power is
not so much of an issue and the swing plane
is naturally steeper. Two-time US Masters
champion José-Maria Olazabal has struggled
with this fault all his career; hence his superb
iron play and notoriously ragged driving.

At the top of your
backswing, your weight
should be on the right.

The weight should then
shift to your left side
through impact.

Missing too many greens

One of the major faults of high-handicap golfers is not so much in their swing as in their club selection. This comes down to knowing your own game and, more importantly, your own yardages.

If you are in the heat of battle and are hitting a number of shots short, then you are probably not taking enough club. Remember that different conditions on different days will make the ball fly further or shorter. If it is hot, the ball will travel far, whereas on a cold winter's morning you may need an extra couple of clubs.

Quick fixes

Be practical
The key is not to be proud. You may hit your 8-iron 128m (140 yd) when you hit it dead centre, but chances are that you won't catch it off the centre of the club every time. So drop to a 7-iron for this distance.

Work out your averages
Now learn your yardages. Spend an hour on the range pacing out how far you hit each club.

1 Hit 20 balls with one club.

2 Ignore the best and worst three shots.

3 Take an average distance from the remaining 14 balls.

4 This is your yardage for that club.

PRO-TIP

When a professional plays an approach shot, they rarely leave the ball short of the hole. Take a club that will fly beyond the flag; this gives it a chance of going in. To help, aim at the top of the flag as opposed to the bottom.

Use your yardages properly
Most courses have yardage signs or indicators – don't ignore these. Invest in a course guide before you start as this will give more accurate distances. Use this reference and trust it as your eyes can mislead you about distances. Are the given yardages for the front or middle of the green? There can be as many as two club's difference between the front and back of the green.

Working out your own yardages and sticking to them leads to a positive swing and will focus your attention on the target.

Stop thinning and fatting irons

Thinning the ball with your iron shots is down to two things:
- **Changing your spine angle during your swing.**
- **Gripping the club too tightly.**

Quick fixes

Cure thin-iron shots
To stop gripping the club too tightly, practise swinging whilst holding the club with only your thumb and the forefinger of both hands. This is how tightly to hold the club when you use a proper grip. Colin Montgomerie says that he holds the club so lightly that you can pull it gently out of his hands.

Cure fat-iron shots
To stop hitting the ball fat, tuck a bag-towel under your right arm. Keep this in place as you take some swings. This will force you to keep your arms close to your body on the downswing and will shorten your swing arc and stop you hitting the ball fat. Hold the towel in place until your arms are fully extended at impact, then let it fall naturally to the ground.

The key is to keep the towel in place until impact, while keeping your arms tight to your body. Extending your arms too early causes fat shots.

Making swings while holding a bag-towel in place under your right arm is a great way of curing persistent fat shots.

EXTRA-THIN IRON CURE

To obtain a consistent spine angle, you must concentrate on keeping the flex in your right knee steady throughout. Place a ball under your right heel at address, then take some practice swings. This will force you to flex your knee through the shot. This drill will also help cure the reverse pivot.

Place a ball under your right heel at address (as above), so that only the ball of your foot is touching the ground.

With the ball in place under your foot, make some practice swings as it will force you to keep the flex in your right knee.

Sloping lies

Here are some tips that should help you when you are stuck on an incline. They will help you to avoid the slippery slope to dropped shots.

Quick fixes

Narrow or widen your stance depending on the slope. Playing from a slope affects leg action in the swing. To practise for uphill lies, a good trick is to hit some full shots from a narrow stance, giving you more movement in the lower half of your body.

Try the opposite for working on downslopes: widen your stance to promote more stability on what is a tricky shot through which to retain your balance.

Practise the situations

Often people ignore the most simple practice rules. You will find your ball in a divot on the course, so the best practice drills are to hit balls out of divots. Similarly, with slopes, find a patch where you can practise hitting shots from above and below your feet. Experiment with clubs to see the different reactions and develop confidence for these awkward situations.

Sloping lies quick reminders

Situation	Effect
Ball above feet.	Likely to drift left.
Ball below feet.	Likely to slide right.
Ball on an upslope.	Loss of distance.
Ball on a downslope.	Gain distance.

By narrowing your stance, you will improve your body movement and this will lead to better all-round ball striking.

KEY SLOPE TIP

The ball will fade and draw from various different lies, as outlined above, but the longer the club, the greater the effect, so aim further left if you have a 4-iron in your hands when the ball is below your feet, and not so far if you are only hitting a pitching wedge.

Stop shanking forever

Here are two fantastic drills to use on the practice range that will iron out your shank. They will not only kill off the shank, but are great for improving your all-round game.

Quick fixes

Two-legs-in-one drill

When you dip your head, you swing over the top, come across the line and might shank. So stand with your feet together or crossed and hit a bucket of balls. From this position it is impossible to lose your height and dip at the ball. With your feet together, you will have to bring the club back to the ball on line, avoiding a shank. Replicate that feeling when you are over the ball.

The obstacle drill

Place an empty golf ball box 2.5cm (1in) outside where the ball would be. Now make some practice swings, aiming to miss the box. Any time that you strike the box, you will have swung from outside the line and would have shanked the ball. Next, actually play some shots, hitting practice balls and concentrating on missing the obstacle of the box. This should help your swing so that you do not shank the ball when playing.

It is impossible to dip your head when your legs are together.

This stance will make you bring the club to the ball on-line.

The obstacle drill will stop you from coming from outside the line towards the ball. If you hit the box, you would have shanked the shot.

Cure the reverse pivot

This debilitating error will erase power and consistency. Here are two drills that will help eradicate the problem. The first is an old classic and the second an innovative idea.

Quick fixes

Pivot drill

This is a good drill for creating power and building a decent shoulder turn, as well as curing the reverse pivot.

1 Adopt your normal posture and place a club behind your shoulders whilst holding on to either end of the club and flex your knees.

2 Coil your upper body around your spine so that the club points towards your right toe – your weight should now be on your back foot. This is the right position for the top of your backswing.

3 Rotate through, simulating the downswing so that the other end of the club points either at or beyond your right foot.

Which weigh?

To carry out this innovative weight shift drill, you need two sets of bathroom scales.

1 Place the scales on the ground and mimic your address with one foot placed on each set of scales. Your weight should be evenly distributed.

2 Swing and hold at the top. Look at the dials – your weight should be 70 per cent on the right.

3 Swing through to a finish and your weight should move to your left.

4 If the left-hand scale increases as you take the club back, you are reverse pivoting. Concentrate on making the left scale drop and the right rise as you swing back.

Take the address position with the club behind your shoulders.

Rotate your upper body around your spine as demonstrated.

Make sure that you have plenty of room to do this drill. A garden or an uncluttered garage is best.

SHORT GAME

Fluffing chips

How many times do you see professional golfers chip it close when they are around the green? They never seem to miss and they roll the ball to within half a metre (a couple of feet) every time. They never mess up the shot so that it dribbles only a metre, or catch the top of the ball, thinning it through the back of the green.

Chipping should be relatively simple. The technique is not as complex as a full-swing, the distances are not as large. So why is it so difficult? Good chipping comes down to confidence. If you are confident, your technique will be solid, your thoughts positive and your ball-striking will be clean.

The best chippers in the world, such as Seve Ballesteros, complement exemplary technique with awesome imagination. They can not only play the most incredible shots, but they can also see them. This is a great skill that you can also develop through practice and experience.

Standing on a green, lobbing balls with your hands, just to see how they react on the putting surface is a great way of nurturing imagination. A positive attitude will also help: look to hole your chips as opposed to simply getting them close. You'll soon stop worrying about fluffing these shots and will be able to use your imagination.

Confidence in your technique leads to flair and imagination around the greens.

✚ On-course first aid and long-term recovery

FIXES	GO TO PAGE
● Fluffed chip	p68
● Thinned chip	p69
● Chipping into, not over, hazards	p74

Inaccurate chipping

Ma~~ybe your~~ trouble with chipping is
... leaking shots
... you often get
... four. You
... ance of an

... times you
... hort or too long,
... tres wide of the
... y to resolve as
... gnment or bad

... touch and
... s, you need to
... e.

Inaccurate chipping is very frustrating and will put your
putting under extra pressure – developing feel is crucial
for saving shots.

On-course first aid and long-term recovery

FIXES	GO TO PAGE
● Leaving it short	p71
● Chipping too far	p72–3
● Chipping right	p72
● Chipping left	p73
● General inaccuracy	p74

Use all the tools in your bag

When chipping, make use of all the clubs at
your disposal. If you are in the fringe around
the green, the grass is likely to snag your club.
Avoid this by chipping with a 3- or 5-wood.
Don't be afraid to use your putter in strange
places – it is often the percentage shot if
there are not any obstacles in your path.

WHAT IS AN 'UP-AND-DOWN'?

Getting 'up-and-down' is holing out in two
shots from any position. It is most commonly
used for chipping and bunker play, where you
chip close and hole a short putt.

Fluffing chips

There is a subtle difference between a fluffed and a thinned chip. A fluffed chip is when you catch the turf before the ball, taking a chunk out of the ground and any speed out of the clubhead, leaving the ball short. You thin the ball when you hit it halfway up, taking no divot at all. This makes the ball fly low and hard past the target.

If you have fluffed the ball and not made any ground forward, you'll be feeling disheartened. The reason for this disappointment is not only where the ball has finished up but also the negative nature of your swing. A fluff like this comes from hesitation in hitting through the ball.

Quick fixes

Short but sweet
A quick way to encourage an acceleration through the ball is to take a shorter backswing but to swing positively towards the target. As your backswing is shorter, you will be trying to hit the ball harder and will naturally accelerate your swing.

You may also have stunted your follow-through, often a clear sign of a deceleration through impact. Think of the chipping stroke as a pendulum that must swing the same distance back as through. If you concentrate on reaching that finishing position, then the ball simply gets in the way of the swing and everything should go smoothly.

Concentrate on the club accelerating through the ball. If you are struggling with this, have a shorter backswing and work on a longer follow-through.

A shorter backswing but long follow-through will help acceleration through the ball.

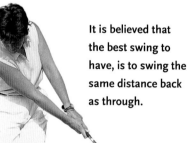

It is believed that the best swing to have, is to swing the same distance back as through.

Thinning the ball through the back

A fluff and a thin are very similar problems. They both come from decelerating through impact. A thin is often more destructive as the ball races across the green, often into trouble beyond the flag, leaving you further away than when you started. A thinned chip may happen because you are trying to loft the ball using your wrists as opposed to the club's loft.

Quick fixes

Return to address

A decent address position for chipping is with the ball back in your stance – opposite your right foot – with your hands forward by your left thigh. When you swing, try to return to that address position at impact. This will keep your wrists firm and let the club do the work. This will also keep the width in your arms. You do not want to move your elbows in the swing, you simply want to keep them as flexed at impact as they were at address. Moving your elbows will lead to topped chips.

Hands ahead throughout

Your hands should start ahead of the club at address and they should stay ahead through the entire swing. Aim to have your hands ahead of the club in your finishing position. This will again take your wrists out of the stroke. Keeping your hands ahead will also help to keep the lower body still as your natural swing will generate power. Lower body movement while chipping can cause problems.

By returning to the address position at impact you will develop a pure and crisp strike with your chipping.

Keep your hands ahead of the club head to the top of the backswing.

Ensure that your hands stay ahead of the club through the whole chip shot.

Inaccurate chips

Feel and control around the greens when chipping is down to a solid technique and decent set-up, but often poor shot selection can scupper these good fundamentals and you can end up hitting the ball too far. Golfers who regularly strike the ball well but way beyond the target, may need to rethink their strategy.

For any chip that you face, there are usually a number of options on how to play it. You can fly the ball to the hole on the full, stop it dead or play a chip-and-run. If you have consistently been hitting the ball too far, you've probably been using the same club for every chip and altering your swing.

Quick fixes

Get the ball rolling
When chipping, get the ball rolling on the green as quickly as possible because it is much easier to judge distance in terms of working out how the ball will roll on the green rather than how it will fly through the air.

If you have 5m (16ft) of fringe green between you and the putting surface, you will not need to loft the ball high in the air and land it by the flag. Similarly, if you are chipping over a bunker to a pin close to the green's edge, there is no room to run the ball. You must use the correct club for the shot but, crucially, you mustn't change your swing.

Lofting the ball to useless heights when there is nothing to carry adds a huge risk as the wind may affect its flight and it will not be as easy to control when it lands.

Change club
For different chip shots, change the club in your hands, not your swing. Changing your technique will lead to inconsistencies in strike through over-complicating the shot.

You may need to carry hazards before the ball can roll on the green.

You must get the ball rolling on the putting surface as quickly as possible.

Leaving the chip short

Often, poor club selection will leave you with a longer putt than you anticipated. Trying to chip-and-run with a sand-wedge will leave you long in 'chip' and short on 'run' but there is another major factor that will leave the ball short. Chipping short can be down to a lack of conviction over the shot.

Quick fix

Clocking on

A great thought to have is the clock face. This will give you something to tune into around the greens and should develop a more positive stroke. As you chip, imagine a clock face behind you and that your hands are the hour hand of the clock. For each different chip shot, you are not going to alter your swing speed but simply the length of your backswing so use this clock face image to control your swing. Your feet are standing at the six on the clock and your head is at twelve. For a 6m (20ft) shot with a 9-iron, as you swing back, your

QUICK CHIP TIP

For any chip, try to picture a spot where you want the ball to land before it rolls up towards the flag. Then, as you prepare for the shot, picture in your mind the ball doing exactly what you want. This gives you a much greater chance of getting close.

hands should go back only far enough to be pointing at the imaginary eight on the clock. Then swing through to the three on the clock. Experiment with different clubs and different 'times' to see what works best for you and how far each shot goes. Then, when you are faced with a tricky short chip, you can feel confident in dialling up the right length of swing. This thought will also make you swing firmly through the ball, as you will be thinking more about what to do than what not to do.

Use the clock face to gauge your chips.

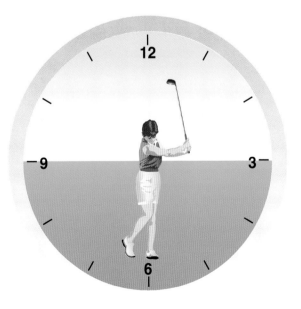

Always make a positive through-swing.

Chipping too far right

If you have at last mastered your distance control, it is infuriating to start chipping off-line. Hitting the ball the right distance but in the wrong direction is no use to anyone. More often than not, chipping too far right or left is down to set-up problems. The best cure for inaccurate chipping, especially when you are chipping right of the target, is a quick address position checklist because in the heat of battle, it is easy to let the fundamentals slip.

Quick fix

Address checklist

? Is my alignment good?
Make sure your hips, feet and shoulders are aligned slightly to the left of the target, with your clubface square.

? Why is the ball going right?
If the ball is going right, you could be too straight, so make sure you are open. Make sure the ball is back in your stance.

? Where should the ball be in my stance?
If the ball is opposite your left foot, or central, it is easier to leak the ball out right. Ensure the ball is close to your right foot.

? Where do my hands go?
Keep your hands forward of the ball at address. You want to keep your hands forward of the clubhead throughout any chip shot.

? How should I have my weight?
Ensure your weight at address is predominantly on your left foot. Too much weight on your back foot could lead to a weak scoop at the ball, pushing it right.

Alignment is vital to chipping – bad alignment can affect your chances of getting up and down.

If you let your ball position slip at address, you could be in trouble and faced with a long putt. Keep the ball back in your stance.

Chipping too far left

Missing a chip to the left of the target can again be down to a faulty set-up but it may also be due to the lie from which the ball came. Also, an in-to-out swing path could put drawspin on the ball, which will drag it leftwards and away from the hole.

Quick fixes

Smoothing out the rough
When you are chipping from thicker rough, the clubhead is likely to snag on the grass at impact. This snag shuts the clubface, making the ball fly left. To overcome this, hit the ball more firmly than if you were playing from a decent lie. Take more loft and concentrate on holding your wrists firm through the shot. If you keep the grip pressure of the last three fingers on your left-hand firm, it will be easier to hold the clubface square.

Follow the correct path
If you feel your swing is making the ball veer left, take a few seconds while waiting on the tee to check your swing path with this quick test:

1 Place a clubshaft on the ground parallel to your ball-to-target line.

2 Take some practice swings.

3 If you hit the shaft on your backswing, you are swinging 'out-to-in'. If you collide with the shaft on your follow-through, the path is 'in-to-out'.

Either of these faults is likely to make the ball go left, but if you are swinging 'in-to-out' you may put some destructive topspin on the ball that drags it further left. You will want to swing along the ball-to-target line, so take some practice swings whilst keeping parallel to the shaft. Replicate that feeling when over the ball.

WHAT'S AN 'IN-TO-OUT' AND AN 'OUT-TO-IN' SWING?

When you hear commentators and fellow golfers discussing such things they are talking about the path the club travels in a swing. 'Out-to-in' means the club is travelling from outside the target line – away from the golfer's body – to inside the line and closer to the golfer. The opposite is true of an 'in-to-out' swing.

Check your chipping swing path by placing a club parallel to the target line.

Inaccurate Chips

To work on the accuracy and consistency of your short game, you must concentrate on two things:
• Solid technique
• Developing feel
There are a number of good practice tips and drills that you'll find invaluable in sharpening your chipping skills.

Quick fixes

Chip from the hardest lie
To improve your ball-striking and to build confidence in a solid technique, try this difficult drill to iron out any flaws. It is so unforgiving that once you've mastered it, normal chips will seem simple. Focus on your address position and return to it at impact.

1 Find an old wedge or 9-iron that you don't mind scratching.

Chipping from a hard surface can really benefit your short-game technique, but make sure you use an old club!

2 Find a path or a slab of concrete next to a green or area on to which you can chip.

3 Hit some chips from this hard lie. Don't worry where the ball finishes; just concentrate on a decent strike.

The ladder drill
To develop the feel for how far your clubs carry and roll try the ladder drill.

1 Place about five clubs on the green 1m (3ft) apart. Drop six balls on the fringe of the green and near the shafts.

2 Starting with a 7-iron, try to land the ball in the gap between the first and second club, then the second and third club, and so on. Keep going until you know how that club reacts with different length swings.

3 Swap clubs to work out how they react. Make a note of the distances and put it to good use when you are in the heat of battle.

Place clubs on the green at equal distances apart so they look like a ladder.

Using different clubs, aim to land balls in the gaps of the ladder.

Getting a feel for chipping

When you try to throw a piece of paper in the bin, you hit it more often than not. When you lob someone a ball, without thinking about it, you throw it close enough to catch. Natural instincts make you throw close, you never let the ball or paper drop out of your hand and land on your feet and you never fling it yards past your target. This is because you have natural feel.

Add some variety to your chipping practice by hitting to different targets dropped around the chipping green. This will not only be interesting but will build-up your natural feel.

Quick fix

Find your natural feel
The same natural feel applies to chipping. Imagine you are lobbing the ball with your hand towards the target. Actually do this on the practice green – lob balls at a target. You will be amazed at how your natural eye gives you a decent feel for the pace and also an instinctive read of the greens.

CHIP OR PITCH?

Many golfers think the difference between these two shots lies in the distances involved – you chip from close, pitch from further away. This is not always accurate. You can play a chip and run from 46m (50yd) on a hard running links, yet may use an accurate pitch to a soft green from 27m (30yd). With a chip, the hands do not go higher than your hips. With a pitch, the hands pass your hips with wrist hinge.

When you are next over a chip, take some practice swings with just your hands. Pretend you are throwing the ball at the hole, then replicate this feel on your chipping stroke.

Picking targets
To sharpen up your versatility around the greens, place four or five bag-towels on the putting surface in different places. Then find a good lie around the green. Take a dozen balls and aim to land them on each towel in turn. Don't continue chipping to the same towel for more than two balls in a row. Keep varying the targets for each chip and mark a score for how close you are. Keep trying to lower your score.

Competitive practice is a great way of sharpening your short game. By inventing games and challenging friends you will improve more quickly than by aimlessly hitting balls.

PUTTING

One of the most frustrating aspects of golf is when you find the putting surface with your approach, then drop a shot through sloppy putting. You can hit the ball brilliantly but a string of three-putts will destroy your round. What's more, three-putting is contagious. Once you have had one or two in a row, your nerve goes and the next 3m (10ft) putt looks like 15m (50ft).

There are a number of different reasons for three-putting but the main reason is a misjudgment of line or pace. To ensure a two-putt at worst from that 3m (10ft) range, line is more important than pace. If you judge the line correctly and are positive with the stroke, you should hole a few and never let one slip by.

THE EQUIPMENT EFFECT

If you want to be a consistent putter, you must have the right tool in your bag. If your putter is too long or short, it will be hard to develop a consistent stroke. A short putter leads to a hunched posture – too long, and you will stand too upright. At address, your hands should be below your shoulders. If you find this difficult, check with your local professional that your putter is right for you.

If you are consistently missing putts, you will be struggling to string a decent run of holes together. The right stroke and the right tool will help to overcome this problem.

✚ On-course first aid and long-term recovery

FIXES	GO TO PAGE
● Can't hit it on-line once read	p80
● No consistency with stroke	p80
● Misreading long putts	p86
● Misreading short putts	p88
● Solid putting forever	p90

Misjudging the length of putts

Judging pace on the greens can be very tricky, particularly if you are playing different courses regularly. There are no physical techniques that will help you find a feel for greens – it is often said that putting is more of an art than a science – but there are some sensible steps you can take and practice techniques that will help you establish the pace of the putting surface quickly.

When faced with a long putt, 6m (20ft) and further, your main priority is to gauge the pace. If you can hit the putt the right distance, you will always be close. You are not expecting to hole-out regularly from this distance, so making the ball reach the hole and stop within 60cm (2ft) is more important than the slight left-to-right break in the middle of the putt.

On-course first aid and long-term recovery

FIXES	GO TO PAGE
● Inconsistency	p80
● General pace problems	p82
● Inconsistent judgment of pace	p84
● Misreading short putts	p88
● Solid putting forever	p90

When faced with a long putt, your major concern should be with pace as opposed to line – getting the ball within a 60cm (2ft) circle around the hole is the aim.

Missing putts left and right

If you have ever sat down and worked out where you miss most putts, the chances are that you have concluded that they have slipped past the right edge of the cup. This is the most common putting problem. Golfers rarely allow enough break on the left side and then watch the ball dribble past the lower right side of the hole.

Perhaps you are not one of the crowd and find you tug them left, taking the break and travelling further left. Either way, you will score low only if the ball has a chance of dropping. If you've missed a few to one side, try these fixes.

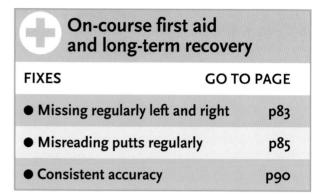

On-course first aid and long-term recovery

FIXES	GO TO PAGE
● Missing regularly left and right	p83
● Misreading putts regularly	p85
● Consistent accuracy	p90

Many golfers do not leave enough break on a putt, leading to missing left and right even when the pace is good.

Missing short putts

Most three-putts involve a missed short one. It can drain you of all your confidence and if you have missed two short putts in a row, the hole begins to seem tiny and your ball even smaller.

If, on the other hand, you have sunk a few medium-range putts in succession, you'll stand up to the next one and knock it in without a second thought. Having confidence over short putts has an effect on the rest of your game and your full swing.

Short putts are a challenge only because the golfer thinks they're tricky. A positive approach can change all that.

On-course first aid and long-term recovery

FIXES	GO TO PAGE
● Missing left	p88
● Missing right	p88
● Leaving putts short	p88
● Missing on both sides	p89
● Short with short putts	p88
● Never miss from close range	p90

Holing regularly from close range keeps a score going and is vital in recovery shots.

Regularly knocking short putts in builds confidence for the rest of your game.

Putting problems

Most putting problems, like most other difficulties in the golf swing, come from problems at address. If a few putts have slipped by, you should make a quick check of your address position, your alignment and your general set-up.

Quick fixes

The ball position
This is vitally important when putting. If your putts are going right, the ball is too far forward. If your putts are going left, the ball is too far back. The ideal ball position for the putting stroke is directly below your eyes. Use this quick check to ensure your ball has not shifted in your stroke:

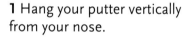

1 Hang your putter vertically from your nose.

2 If the putterhead covers the ball, you are in the correct position.

With your eyes over the ball, you will have a much better view of the line of the putt.

Perfect your posture
Missing can be because of weak posture as posture affects the consistency of your ball-striking. These are the basics of good putting posture:

1 Attain athletic angles at address.

2 Bend from the hips keeping your back straight.

3 Keep your hands under your shoulders, not outside or near your thighs.

GET A GRIP ON YOUR PUTTING

If you have no control on your putts from distance, it is probably because of a poor grip. Your grip is your one connection with the club. If it is not comfortable then good 'feel' is impossible. Start by using an orthodox, reverse overlap, grip and if this doesn't work, try one of the numerous ways of holding the putter. These are the three most famous:

1 Reverse overlap is the most orthodox technique and is generally regarded as the easiest way of controlling the putterhead.

2 Left-below-right is a technique that will level your shoulders at address and produce a shallow stroke, which can lead to a much purer, more consistent strike.

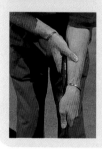

3 The Langer grip is not that common and was devised by Bernhard Langer after a serious bout of the yips. It is best to use this as a last resort.

4 Use a small amount of knee flex.

5 Keep your arms slightly bent, with your elbows pointing towards the ribcage.

Get your alignment straight

Putts not starting on the chosen line can be due to poor alignment. Starting with your body aligned correctly will help you obtain a consistent strike. Check that all the crucial points are parallel to your chosen ball-to-target line. Some teachers suggest a slightly open stance is okay, but staying parallel leaves nothing to chance.

Quick fixes

Alignment checklist

- Are your feet parallel?
- Are your knees parallel?
- Are your shoulders parallel?
- Is your putterhead square to target?

Keep the same address

If you are changing your set-up for different lengths of putts, you are doing yourself no favours. You need to keep your address position consistent so that your stroke is consistent. The only thing that should change is how far back you take the putterhead. Other than that, the set-up is the same for a 10m (35ft) putt as it is for one 2m (6ft) away.

Good alignment means having everything square to the target line.

No matter what length the putt is, the alignment should remain the same.

AIM THE LOGO ON YOUR LINE

This is a great way to square your putterface to your ball-to-target line at address. Mark your ball or use the manufacturer's logo to point straight at the intended target line. Set the putter square to this and take your stance. Once you are lined up, it is easy to take a smooth, square stroke.

Putting problems

Once you have a solid set-up, the next thing to worry about is your stroke. The length of stroke determines how far the putt will travel. There are some common mistakes which affect your feel for length over long range.

Quick fix

Equidistant back and through

For a solid putting stroke that gives you greatest feel, you must establish a rhythm with some practice strokes and stick to it. The only thing that changes is the length of your backswing. The further you want to strike the putt, the further back you take the club. Once you have taken the club back, to avoid leaving it short, you must take it the same distance through. Here is a great positive thought that will stop you leaving it short more often than not: 'Long back – long through.'

If you are struggling to find decent feel on the greens, you are probably taking the club back short and fast, causing a jabbing stroke. With this type of stroke, it is hard to develop good feel.

A good, long stroke encourages you to accelerate through the ball, making it roll on a purer line and not deviate as much.

ENLARGE THE HOLE

If you are struggling for feel from distance, picture the hole as a dustbin lid. You want to stop the ball in this 1-metre-wide (3-feet-wide) dustbin lid. This positive thought should help you leave yourself easy shots as opposed to nerve-janglers.

To help develop a consistent feel on your longer putts, work on perfecting a longer backswing in the stroke.

Concentrate on swinging through as far as you swung back, to fight against deceleration.

Missing putts left and right

If you are missing long putts on either side of the cup, it may be because you are struggling to keep your putting stroke on-line. Try these on-course thoughts.

Quick fixes

Too much wrist action

In the putting stroke, you must have no wrist action. Think 'Y': the shaft of your club and your arms should form a 'Y' shape. Keep the putter low to the ground as you swing the club away with your arms and shoulders – not your wrists – and keep that 'Y'. Accelerate smoothly through the ball, keeping your 'Y' and not using any wrist action.

The grandfather clock

If you are missing putts right, you could well be cutting across the ball with an out-to-in swing path. This is a result of too much lower body movement. You must keep your legs and bottom still throughout the putting stroke – just move your shoulders. Think of your shoulders, arms and putterhead as the pendulum of the grandfather clock and of your body as the outer casing. The casing of the grandfather clock never moves as the pendulum swings – this is how your putting stroke should be.

Establish good wrist angle at address.

Keep this wrist angle on your backstroke.

Hold that wrist angle at the finish position.

You are the grandfather clock. Your arms and putter form the pendulum, while your body is the casing, which does not move.

DIFFERENT STROKES FOR DIFFERENT FOLKS

It is important to remember that there is no right or wrong way of putting. If you analyzed the best putters in the world, you would reveal an assorted mix of techniques, grips, putters and strokes – none of which is any worse than the other. American Billy Mayfair has made a fortune from taking the putter back outside the line. As always, though, having decent fundamentals will give you the best chance.

Getting the right feel for putting

Putting is the most rewarding and depressing part of the game. Part of the problem is that it can be rewarding at one hole and then depressing at the next one. To develop consistent feel and ball striking, you need to develop a consistent routine.

A BUBBLE OF CONCENTRATION

A decent routine is critical when you are playing pressure putts. It is the bubble of concentration into which you can retreat when the heat is on. Make it become second nature through hard practice on the green – it should feel odd to putt without it. Stick to your routine for every putt, however long.

Quick fix

A matter of routine

If you are having mixed fortunes on the greens, quickly develop a short routine. Here are the crucial elements of a good routine:

- Reading the putt.
- Taking practice strokes.
- Taking one last look.
- Pulling the trigger.

1 Read the putt from two different angles: behind the hole and behind the ball.

2 Take three practice strokes while looking at the hole. Make your practice stroke the stroke you use for real.

3 Address the ball and take a last look at the hole.

4 Look back to the ball and take the putter away within two seconds.

Rescue your putting by developing an emergency on-course routine, which can be refined later.

A permanent putting routine

Once you have rescued your round with a basic routine, it is time to get on the practice green and develop a more detailed, but equally quick, pre-shot putting preparation routine. You should already have the skeleton of a routine (from page 84) with the crucial elements in place. Here are some extra hints to make it even sharper. Remember, if you take too long, you will infuriate partners and other golfers, so keep it short and proficient.

Quick fix

A matter of routine

1 Read the putt as you walk up to the green, as this will save time.

2 Take your practice strokes looking at the hole.

This will make better use of your natural feel, which we all have.

3 Your routine should take exactly the same time to complete, from reading the putt to pulling the trigger, for every putt you hit, whether it is your first putt of the round or a 3m (10ft) putt to halve the match. This should not be a long period of time.

4 Walk into the putt along the line in which you intend to start the ball; not in a direct line between you and the hole. This again helps develop your natural touch.

5 Do not freeze over the putt or all the preparation you have done will be lost. Lee Trevino had a great expression: 'If you are going to miss a putt, miss it quickly.'

0 secs

Make sure you read your putts from at least two different angles.

10 secs

Your practice swings are the same strokes used when playing the shot for real.

15 secs

The routine should take exactly the same amount of time ... every time.

Reading putts

Deciphering the line and break of a putt is an art in itself. To some talented golfers it comes naturally; to others it requires a great deal of practice and experience. If you are struggling to read the greens, you could do worse than absorb the eight best tips from around the golfing world.

Quick fixes

The best-ever tips for reading putts

1 Look for the clues. There are clues all around you when you're reading a putt. Tiger Woods will always look for the highest peak – putts will break away from this. Putts break towards water, so if you are on a lakeside green, aim away from the hazard.

2 If you are putting uphill, you will have to hit the ball harder so that the break is less pronounced. When putting downhill, the break will be exaggerated. The same is true with slow and fast greens – fast greens break more than slow ones.

3 You need to worry about the break only over the last third of a long putt. The subtle undulations in the green will not affect it early on as you will have hit the putt so firmly. Take practice swings from where the break will take hold to decipher the read more clearly.

4 Pour water to find the break. Payne Stewart used to imagine that he was pouring a bucket of water on top of the grass and then pictured which way it would run to find a good read.

There are clues everywhere when it comes to reading putts – make clue-hunting part of your pre-shot routine.

5 Over long putts, professional golfers will give the putt more room than they initially think, by a few metres. If they miss the putt, they want to miss on the high side, so that the ball is always dying towards the hole. Occasionally, they will get lucky and one will drop.

6 If you have trouble hitting along the break you have chosen, treat every putt as a straight putt. Aim at where you think the break will take hold; this may be at right-angles to where the hole is, and set-up straight to this 'apex'. Then make a confident stroke.

THE CURSE OF SLOW PLAY

Every golfer should have a pre-shot routine before putting but this is not an excuse to play slowly. Amateur golfers are on the course for fun and relaxation even if it is a serious monthly medal. Take the same, short time over each putt and do not copy the professionals' lengthy preparations. Many commentators believe they have taken this aspect of the game to excess but they are playing for vast sums of money – even in your grudge match, the stakes are not that high.

Treating every putt as a straight one and hitting at the apex of the break takes the fear out of breaking putts.

7 Before you make your putt, picture in your mind's eye the ball rolling towards the hole and taking the break you've chosen. If you have any doubts, trust the first impressions you had about the break when you arrived on the green, as these are usually right.

8 Once you are over the putt and have taken your last look at the hole, trust the read you've made. Often putts will look different when you are over the ball and you second guess yourself. Don't do this. Trust your read and make a positive strike.

Missing short putts

If you have pulled the ball left of the hole, a common cause is lifting your head and shoulders through impact. This is usually because you are anxious over the putt and want to see where it has gone.

Missing right is the most common problem with short putts, as it comes from the clubface not returning to the ball square at impact, and consequently spinning the ball right. This is easy to do if you are not confident with your stroke.

Worse than missing left or missing right is leaving putts short. If you have left a 2m (6ft) putt short, you have committed the cardinal sin in golf. This is a putt you should hole and you have not even given it a chance.

Quick fixes

Missing left
Staying down through the ball is important over this short distance. When you are over a 2m (6ft) putt, keep looking at where the ball

Think only about your follow-through if you are missing a number of short putts – make sure you finish with your putterhead swinging towards the target.

was until you hear the rattle in the bottom of the cup. Nick Faldo was a great exponent of listening to the drop. Watch footage of his Open Championship win at Muirfield in 1992 – even over the final 0.5m (2ft) putt when the title is his, he never sees the ball go in the hole. He just listens to the rattle then takes the applause.

Missing right
Colin Montgomerie says that he misses putts right if he has not taken the putter back far enough – this is often the case with amateurs. If you have a short backswing, you are in danger of losing your rhythm and a short backswing allows your hands to get ahead of the ball and push it right. So, if you are blocking putts, use a few seconds to practise taking the putter back a touch further.

Leaving short putts short
With shorts putts of this length, you are trying to hole the ball, so think aggressively. When you have picked a line for the putt – and only on rare occasions should you be aiming outside the hole – concentrate on your follow-through. Don't think about how you took the club back or how you struck the ball; concentrate on finishing with your putterhead swinging towards the target.

This simple thought will encourage you to be positive.

Missing on both sides

Missing a short putt either right or left can often be down to misreading the line. There are a number of tips and hints on how to get a decent read but if you are faced with a short putt, your best bet is to ignore them all. Watch Tiger Woods, Sergio Garcia or any younger golf star. They never miss from this range because they hit their putts so firmly.

The harder you hit a 2m (6ft) putt the less you have to worry about the break. If you are in doubt over the read, aim at the middle of the hole and strike the putt firmly. You don't need to worry about the one coming back, because the more positive you are with your stroke, the more likely you are to hole it.

The yips is an odd and dangerous affliction.

THE YIPS

A disabling 'condition' that can reduce a champion golfer to an also-ran and brave men to tears. Often induced by pressure, the communication between the brain and hands breaks down, leaving golfers, in extreme cases unable to take the club back. Causes are unclear.

One thing is certain, it requires heavy putting-green time to cure, but it can be overcome. Bernhard Langer has defeated the yips three times. But if they strike when you are on the course, there is no escape and you have to piece together a round from within your broken putting stroke. Try changing your putting grip. This is how Langer recovered in the long-term.

Quick fixes

Beating the yips

If you have never heard of the yips before, you are very lucky. This is a severe and strange problem that can affect the most talented golfers. When faced with a short putt, the golfer inexplicably flinches at the ball, with an almost spasmodic flick of the wrists. The stroke is involuntary and the ball is out of control, often finishing far from the hole. Many of the greatest golfers have suffered from this ignoble and severe problem. It is a real disorder, like a disease, and there is on-going research in the United States trying to work out the cause.

Try a new grip in order to soothe the yips.

You may have to practise the yips away.

Putting solidly forever

Three-putting is best overcome on the practice green. You can work on your stroke and technique but when it comes to regular two-putts, you will have to work on your feel and never missing from 2m (6ft). The best way to do this is through putting drills. These not only make practice more fun but also help your game immeasurably.

Quick fixes

Blindfold drill

If you have lost your touch from range or are playing a number of different courses and need to figure out the pace of the putting surface quickly, this is the perfect drill because it cuts out one of your senses (your sight) to improve the others and is widely used by professionals around the world.

The blindfold drill is great for developing feel.

1 Take three or four balls and give yourself a 5m (15ft) putt. Take your address position over one of the balls.

2 Shut your eyes and putt at the hole.

3 Before you open your eyes, guess where your ball finished and then look to see how wrong you were.

4 Keep putting with your eyes shut. You will find your touch improves and you'll be guessing accurately and gauging the pace of the ball well.

Looking practice

A similar drill to help you fine-tune your touch on the green, and one that is equally as effective, is to take a number of practice putts while looking at the hole but not at the ball. This will train your mind to translate what it sees – the distance of the putt and lie of the land – into a putting stroke.

Putting while looking at the hole also helps to develop feel.

Concentrate on trying to stop the ball in the 1m (3ft) 'safe zone' beyond the hole. This gives the ball a chance of going in but does not leave you too much work back. You can place a club behind the hole to use as a guide for this excellent feel drill.

Tennis ball drill

If you have lost confidence with short putts and find you are leaking shots in your round because of this, a great way to practise is by putting with a tennis ball, rather than a golf ball. This is more difficult than it sounds because to hole a 2m (6ft) putt with a tennis ball you have to hit the ball into the middle of the hole. Once you have done this for a short time, try putting with a proper golf ball – the hole will seem vast and the ball tiny; just what you need to hole short putts. If you practise like this for ten minutes before teeing-off, it will save you at least three shots a round.

Shaft practice

If you find that your shorter putts are either running out of steam before you reach the hole or are dribbling off-line at the end of the putt to miss by the side, you are simply not striking the ball positively enough. As the ball runs out of energy, so the break of the green affects it more. The more firmly you strike the shorter putts, the less you have to worry about the break.

To practise a positive stroke from this range, simply lie a club in front of the hole. Then try to knock in 2m (6ft) putts over this club. You will have to strike the ball more firmly to jump the shaft and you will have to worry less about the break of the putt. You will find the ball pops up and over the shaft before dropping into the hole. To make sure it bounces up and back straight, you will have to hit the putt firmly. Make this an on-course habit.

Build confidence on short putts by practising with a tennis ball.

Become positive with the shaft practice.

HAZARDS

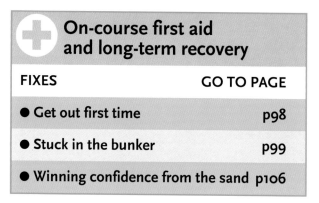

Greenside bunkers

It is infuriating to watch the top players splash the ball from the sand to 1m (3ft), and closer, regularly, especially when you find that when you land in a bunker you write off at least a couple of shots. Bunkers are not the evil monsters they might first appear. Once you get the hang of them, you may prefer to have a sand shot than a chip from a fluffy lie because you can get more control and spin from a bunker. Firstly, though, you have to get out.

✚ On-course first aid and long-term recovery

FIXES	GO TO PAGE
● Get out first time	p98
● Stuck in the bunker	p99
● Winning confidence from the sand	p106

Splashing out close is not the toughest part of the sport it is made out to be.

Gaining control from a bunker

You may be able to escape the trap in one shot but you have no idea where the ball will finish. Sometimes it flies 6m (20ft) past the flag; sometimes it just creeps out, landing 3m (10ft) short. You also knock it dead once in a while.

This is frustrating but can be easily put right with a couple of technical checks and some practice. Finding touch and feel out of the bunkers comes from solid technique, so sort that out first.

Bunkers are the most definitive feature on a golf course, so it was no surprise that the sand inspired one of golf's greatest sayings. On his way to winning the US Open, Gary Player holed from the bunker. An astounded spectator said how lucky the South African was to claim the title. The eight-time major winner replied: 'You know, it's amazing: the harder I practise the luckier I get.'

✚ On-course first aid and long-term recovery

FIXES	GO TO PAGE
● Distance control from the sand	p100
● Splashing out off-line regularly	p101
● Refine a consistent feel	p106

Solid technique from the sand will lead to greater control.

A CONFIDENCE BOOSTER

Out of all the shots you can play in golf, the standard bunker-shot is the most forgiving. You don't have to hit the ball and the equipment is so specially designed for the shot that, used properly, you'll escape the sand and land within putting range regularly. So attack this hazard positively, and you will soon learn that the terror of sand is a myth.

Fairway bunkers

Landing in a fairway bunker will often cost you a shot but it should never cost you more than that. The 70m (80yd) bunker shot is regarded as the most difficult in golf because of its awkward in-between distance.

As a rule, escaping from these traps is never too tricky as they tend to have shallow lips, unless you're on some brutal links course on the British coast. It is making ground from bunkers, as opposed to merely escaping from them, that is more difficult and needs care.

➕ On-course first aid and long-term recovery

FIXES	GO TO PAGE
● Failing to get far from a bunker	p102
● Dealing with fairway bunkers	p102
● Building bunker confidence	p106

THE GREATEST BUNKER SHOT EVER?

Fairway bunkers produce their fair share of drama. In fact, one of the greatest shots ever played was from a fairway bunker. Scotland's Sandy Lyle, perhaps one of the best ball-strikers to have played the game, needed a birdie on the final hole of the Masters in 1988. This is a particularly brutal hole – directly uphill, long, with an ice-rink for a green. Sandy found the left fairway bunker from the tee. Making par from here would be an achievement. But the ball was lying well and the Scot used all his natural ability to strike the purest 7-iron of his career to 3m (10ft) away from the flag, from where he sank the putt to claim the title. Pure magic.

Coping effectively with fairway bunkers is about setting yourself realistic targets. Can you really reach the green?

Coping with horrific lies

As if finding a bunker is not bad enough luck, you then discover that the golfing gods have thrown in a plugged lie, a nasty lip or a bunker slope to contend with. You feel sunk, deflated and generally at odds with the world.

Rather than moping about your loss of good fortune, have some confidence, flex your muscles and prepare to be aggressive as you blast your way out of trouble. Bad lies are only as bad as your next shot.

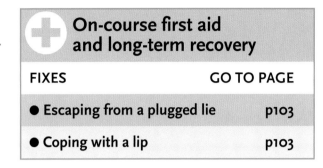

On-course first aid and long-term recovery

FIXES	GO TO PAGE
● Escaping from a plugged lie	p103
● Coping with a lip	p103

As with tough lies from the rough or awkward lies on the fairway, something that golfers never do is practise escaping from plugged lies in the sand.

Bury a dozen balls in a trap and bash them out. You will be surprised at how consistent the ball flight and reaction is and you could well develop your own techniques for escaping.

THE GOLDEN BUNKER RULE

However tough a bunker shot you face, however lacking in confidence you are, however miserable you may feel, focus on the aim of bunker play: escaping in one shot. You may end up yards from the flag but at least you will be back in play and with a better chance of rescuing the hole by holding a long putt or chip.

Plugged lies in bunkers are a nasty part of the game, but good technique and a quick practice session can overcome them well.

Distance control from the rough

There are two types of rough on most courses: the first and second cuts. The first cut of rough is usually bearable and for high handicappers can be preferable, as the ball sits up on a nice cushion of grass.

The second cut is more angry. Physically stronger golfers have the advantage out of the thickest rough as they can blast the ball through the entangling foliage to safety. Escaping is one thing, finding control another.

On-course first aid and long-term recovery

FIXES	GO TO PAGE
● Gaining control from the rough	p104
● Playing safe from the rough	p104

Finding control from the rough is random at the best of times, but with some practice and experience you can make a good guess at how the ball will react.

Finding accuracy from thick lies

The rough can become an entangling graveyard that makes it very difficult to decipher where the ball will finish once you've swiped at it.

There is one thing you always need, though, from any tough lie and that is a bit of luck. Ask Mark Calcavecchia, the 1989 Open Champion. During the final round at Royal Troon he had found himself in a tough spot above the green, with sand between him and the hole. You might say the pressure got to him, but he decelerated into the back of the ball, caught it too thin and watched it skim out low towards the hole. It hit the cup on the full and stayed in for a birdie. The American went on to win the event in a four-way play-off. At that moment, he must have known it was his lucky day.

DON'T DOUBLE THE TROUBLE

When in difficulty, whether you are in the trees, thick rough or nasty bunkers, think 'make bogey my worst score'. If you have to chip out sideways to give yourself a shot to the green, do it. Take your medicine, take your bogey and don't go for that one in ten hero shot that will land a 12 on the card.

✚ On-course first aid and long-term recovery

FIXES	GO TO PAGE
● Accuracy from the rough	p105
● Consistency from the long stuff	p105

To escape successfully from trouble spots you must have a positive swing and attitude, otherwise you are sunk.

Bunker problems

Playing from the sand is an awkward business. The good news is that unlike a standard golf swing, where practice will gently improve your game, changes to your bunker technique can make an automatic difference. If you are struggling to escape the sand, check that you are you starting correctly.

Quick fixes

Set-up checklist to work out if you are addressing the ball properly:

? Where do you position the ball?
For a standard greenside bunker-shot, the ball should be opposite your left heel – forward in your stance.

? How do you get the alignment right?
Align left of the target, to aid the correct swing plane through the ball.

? What do I do with my feet?
Shuffle your feet a few centimetres (inches) into the sand to obtain a secure base, to find a feel of how the sand is lying and to lower your swing arc, which makes it easier to splash out.

? What should the grip be like?
Open the clubface before you take your grip. Some golfers open the clubface for a splash shot but take up their grip and then turn the wrists to open it. This gives you a strong grip and will lead to you digging into the sand, and the ball will travel only a metre (yard) or two forward.

OPENING THE FACE OF THE CLUB BEFORE ADOPTING YOUR GRIP

Try this quick grip drill:
1 Hold the sand-wedge in front of you in your right hand so that it is square.

2 Twist the grip to the right through your fingers so the face opens.

3 Add your left hand and readjust your right to your normal grip.

If you've worked on your set-up, you are confident it is good, and you are still not getting out of bunkers first-time, then your swing may have a few flaws in it.

Quick fixes

Swinging properly
Once you have adjusted your set-up, you must not swing at the target. If you do this you could shank the ball back into the sand, and if you do make good contact, you will end up right of the target. Swing along the line of your feet. With your open face, the club should slide underneath the ball, popping it gently on to the green.

Accelerate through the ball
The biggest cause of non-escape from bunkers is hesitancy in the swing, which leads to deceleration through the ball. The club will either catch the ball thin, driving it into the front of the bunker, or catch it fat, leaving it in the sand.

Think of your swing length. Take the club three-quarters of the way back and make sure you swing to the same distance on the way through. This one key thought will help you accelerate through the ball.

Aim to the left of the target with the clubface open and the ball forward in your stance.

Concentrate on taking the club three-quarters back and swinging the same through.

Accelerate through the ball to a positive finish to ensure that you clear the sand.

No distance control from bunkers

Finding your bunker control is down to practice and technique. Most golfers lose control from the sand when they get too upright at address. This stems from nerves and a lack of confidence. You should also avoid taking the club behind your body in the bunker as this will shut the clubface and lead to an inconsistent strike.

Quick fixes

Staying too upright
Being too upright at address is all wrong and will not give you much control. Tension makes you keen to dig into the sand, rather than splash through it, which will produce an inconsistent strike. To cure this:

1 Have some knee flex at address.

2 Straight knees leads to a 'heavy' upper body so lower your centre of gravity by flexing your knees to lift your chest.

3 If your arms are caught underneath your body, lifting your chest should free them.

Swinging too steeply
To avoid swinging too steeply, it is important not to take the sand-wedge behind your body. So keep this simple thought in mind: 'Keep hands in front of myself throughout the swing.' This will stop you digging into the ball and will make the most of the sand-wedge's design, lifting the ball free from the hazard.

Have some flex at address so you do not hunch over the ball.

Stay upright through the swing, keeping your chest up.

Keep your hands in front of your body throughout your swing.

Always going right or left from bunkers

If you are escaping from bunkers regularly but not getting up-and-down often enough, your accuracy could be wayward. Poor alignment and confused messages on bunker technique can lead to an inaccurate shot.

Quick fixes

Missing right from bunkers
The correct bunker set-up position is with the clubface square to the target and your stance open (aligned left). It is easy to let the clubface fan too far open so check that the clubface is square to the target. If you align your feet to the left of the target, you must also align your shoulders left. It is easy to leave your shoulders behind, keeping them square. You are then likely to swing down your shoulder line, straight at the target, with an open face pushing the ball right. The key is therefore to align yourself left of the target, have your shoulders, knees and feet aiming in this direction, but keep your clubface square to the flag.

CHOKE DOWN FOR ALL BUNKER SHOTS

Gripping down on the club gives you greater control of the clubhead and a better feel for what it is doing. If you tried to eat by holding the top of the knife and fork, it would be more difficult than holding nearer the base – the same is true for a golf club, so for greater control grip near the base of the club.

Missing left from bunkers
Missing bunker shots left often comes from the clubface closing at impact. This could be down to overactive hands releasing too much through the shot. A good way to overcome this is to think of the back of your left hand. You want it to face the sky throughout the shot from start to finish.

Keep your shoulders, knees and feet aligned left of the target, but the club square.

Focus on keeping the back of your left hand facing skyward through the whole shot.

No distance from fairway bunkers

The most common problem from a fairway bunker is not hitting the ball far enough. Fairway bunker technique is similar to that for a normal shot and should be approached in this way, but finding the distance from fairway sand is always tricky. The simple problem with fairway bunkers is that the sand slows the clubhead down. When you strike the ball naturally, taking the equivalent in sand of a grass divot, energy is driven into the sand and not the ball, resulting in a weak shot out.

The club that you ought to use from a fairway bunker depends on two things: how far you are from the green and the height of the lip of the bunker. You will want to take one extra, or longer, club from the fairway bunker than you would from an equivalent distance on the fairway. But you must make sure you have enough loft on the club to clear the lip of the bunker and guarantee an escape. Escaping the sand in one shot is always the priority.

FAIRWAY BUNKER WARNING

Take these precautions:
1 Use an extra club for distance but one with enough loft to clear the lip.
2 Do not shuffle your feet into the sand at all.
3 Set the ball back in your stance.
4 Grip down the club.
5 Think: 'Better thin than fat.'

Quick fix

The most effective tip in golf
From fairway bunkers, grip the club tighter. Try to catch the ball completely clean. When you grip the club tightly, you contract the muscles in your arms. This shortens your swing and makes it almost impossible to take a sand divot.

Grip the club tighter at address.

A good, tight grip will make your swing arc shorter.

The correct grip will mean you catch it more thin than fat.

Always make a full, positive, swing through.

Trouble from troubled lies

Escaping from the sand can become just that — escaping. In bad situations all you want to do is get out of the trap, unless you are Ernie Els, who miraculously gets it close as well.

Quick fixes

Escaping from a plugged lie
When the ball is buried deep in the sand, you should square everything up.

1 Use a pitching-wedge instead of a sand-wedge. Address the ball so that you are parallel to the ball-to-target line and not aligned left (open).

2 Have the ball back in your stance, opposite your right heel. Hinge your wrists as soon as you take the club back.

3 Hit into the sand firmly with a steep swing, using the leading edge of the club to strike 5–8cm (2–3in) behind the ball. Don't worry about your follow-through — your priority is to get the ball out!

Coping with a lip
When you are stuck with a lip on your backswing, hinge your wrists early. Have the ball back in your stance and hit steeply into the back of it.

If you are up against the front lip, place the ball forward in your stance and have your weight on your right. Use the most lofted club you have. The secret of a clean strike is keeping your balance.

This is an awful shot so do not shy away from the bail-out option of chipping out sideways.

This is one of the toughest shots you will have to play.

Keep a steady balance throughout your swing.

Hit at the ball as hard as you can.

Don't worry about a follow-through.

No control from the semi-rough

Many high and mid-handicappers enjoy the fluffy rough, where the ball sits up, making it easier to hit, but distance control from this lie can be difficult. It can lead to you hitting a flyer, where the clubface traps grass between it and the ball. This means the grooves on the club cannot impart the spin on the ball that they normally do. With no spin, the ball not only runs further when it lands but also flies further through the air and can end up going well past your target and into trouble again.

Quick fix

Controlling the flyer
The best way of controlling a flyer is to take a club less than you'd normally use for the distance in question. If there is wind behind you or the course is running particularly quickly, you may want to take two clubs less. The flyer can explode your ball way past the target.

Be careful to guard against the flyer when there is trouble through the back of the green. If it is best to miss by being short, then don't risk firing at the flag.

Flyers can also be friends if you are way back from the green, so always weigh up the options that are available.

The flyer happens when grass is caught between the club and the ball, stopping any spin from being imparted.

HITTING FROM ROUGH TO ROUGH TO ROUGH?

If you find you are never escaping from the thick stuff, then you are most probably suffering a course management breakdown. If you have a tough lie, do not try the glory shot because you saw Seve Ballesteros do it to win the Open Championship at Birkdale in 1979. Chip your ball back on to the fairway to set up the chance of rescuing par and the safety of dropping only one shot.

No accuracy from the rough

When you are fighting out of the jungle, it is often tricky to know how the ball will react when it escapes the foliage. Shots out of even the lighter stuff do tend to fly left of the target, especially if you have not got the most powerful swing or are not the most powerful golfer.

Quick fixes

Strong-arm tactics
The clubhead can get snagged and entangled by grass before impact and this tugs it left and out of line. To compensate for this:

1 Open the clubface at address to allow for the clubhead turning.

2 Grip tightly with your left hand.

3 Aim right of the target.

4 Swing hard – this is one of the few shots in golf where strength in the swing helps.

Thick rough pointers

1 Use the most lofted club in your bag – you want to have the ball airborne as soon as possible. Get the ball nearer your right foot.

2 Set extra weight on your left side at address to make your swing steeper.

3 Swing down firmly on the back of the ball and don't worry about an elegant follow-through.

Place the ball back in your stance – 'right foot for rubbish'.

Swing hard into the back of the ball with all your power.

Don't worry about an elegant follow-through – just focus on escaping.

Building bunker confidence

Once you are confident in your technique and in your ability to escape, then touch and feel will follow quickly. When you next find five minutes for bunker practice, try one of these four drills to improve your confidence in the sand.

Quick fixes

Setting up accurately

To practise a decent set-up, try this technique:

1 Draw a circle in the sand with a 30cm (12in) radius around the ball.

2 Address the ball so that the edge of the circle is near your toes.

3 Open your clubface to add loft. It will aim right at this point.

4 Walk anti-clockwise around the circle until the blade is square.

5 Now take your natural grip of the club and you will have an accurate set-up.

Hitting the line

To lift the ball out of the bunker on a cushion of sand, you have to hit the sand at least 5cm (2in) behind the ball. To build confidence in striking the sand where you want to, take an address position and draw a line in the sand with your fingers. Swing to hit the sand and continue doing this without a ball. You will build confidence and clubhead control.

A good tip when playing a bunker-shot is to focus on the sand at least 5cm (2in) behind the ball as you take the club back. Ignore the ball and look at the sand.

Set up accurately by drawing a circle in the sand.

Move round the circle keeping the clubface square. Inset: build confidence by hitting a practice line in the sand.

Draw a circle with a 5cm (2in) radius around the ball.

Practise hitting the circle and missing the ball to improve your sand-play.

Circles in the sand

Practise taking the correct amount of sand from the bunker by drawing a circle with a 5cm (2in) radius around the ball. Instead of hitting at the ball, hit through the small circle. You will soon learn how the ball floats out of the trap and will feel more confident in your swing, which can only lead to a more positive impact on your game.

Fairway bunker practice

To learn how to catch the ball cleanly out of fairway bunkers, where you are looking to hit the ball thin as opposed to fat (or ideally have a completely clean strike), try this practice routine:

1 Use a fairway bunker with a low lip and a good covering of sand.

2 Place a number of balls in a line of sand stretching away from you.

3 Address the first ball and hit a shot with a full swing.

4 Have a look at the mark you left in the sand; if it is a large mark, this means you have caught the ball heavy.

5 Keep drilling balls but don't worry about the target. Concentrate instead on leaving a small scuff mark in the sand.

6 Place the ball further back in your stance and choke down on the club or grip it tighter to find the right contact.

COURSE MANAGEMENT

There is one thing that all golfers, whatever their standard, have in common – first-tee nerves. That paralyzing, stomach-churning, dark experience of standing on the first tee, terrified of what might happen.

First-tee nerves strike everyone, irrespective of how good they are or what event it is.

First-tee nerves

They may descend upon you because of an intimidating opening hole or maybe you are teeing off in front of a crowd waiting to play behind you. You may imagine a host of faces pressed against the clubhouse window, ready to collapse in mirth at your efforts. Regardless of the cause, first-tee nerves are deeply uncomfortable but they need to be controlled and turned to your advantage, rather than destroyed.

Nerves are part of the sport, and whether you are teeing up in your mate's beer match or playing a pro-am alongside Nick Faldo, nerves will be there. A comforting thought, however, is that no matter who you are, nerves will strike. All top golfers say they feel jittery before teeing up, whatever the event and whatever the round.

Most professional sportsmen are worried if they are not nervous before a game. Nerves sharpen the mind, prepare the body and get the blood flowing. A nerveless sportsman is an empty shell. Embrace rather than fear first-tee nerves: and remember, what really is the worst that can happen?

On-course first aid and long-term recovery

FIXES	GO TO PAGE
● Dealing with first-tee nerves	p112
● How to channel nervous energy	p118

Coping with golf's ups and downs

Dealing with the highs as well as the lows is part of scoring well.

Following a bogey with a bogey is infuriating – a round with no dropped shots suddenly features two or three in a row. Your scorecard is slowly disappearing off the edge of a depressing cliff to land amidst a clatter of bogeys and double-bogeys.

MANAGEMENT SKILLS

Behaving properly on the course is not just about rules and etiquette – it is also about how you behave internally. Most PGA professionals will say that they can save any mid-handicapper five shots a round without touching their swing but by improving their management of the course. This involves shot selection, round organization and general on-course welfare. Good managerial skills are essential to good golf.

Coping with the downs of the round is just as important as coping with the ups. You might open with birdie, par, par and then hole your second shot at the fourth – you're starting to think about the course record and unparalleled praise. A string of mistakes leads to an ordinary round because you have not dealt with the highs well enough. Here are some tips to help you stay in the present and finish the job.

✚ On-course first aid and long-term recovery

FIXES	GO TO PAGE
● Bad hole leads to worse hole	p113
● Ruining a run of good shots with a blow-out	p114
● The art of course management	p119

Starting and finishing badly

How many times do you hear in the clubhouse: 'I would have had my record round, if I hadn't started so badly' or 'I was on for a great score as I walked on to the 16th tee'.

The beginning and end of a round are crucial. The opening hole sets the tone for the day. If it is a double-bogey, it will be an uphill battle; a birdie and you start on a high. You also have to finish the job off once you are on the home stretch – it is easy to let a tired mind and body drop crucial shots.

✚ On-course first aid and long-term recovery

FIXES	GO TO PAGE
● Starting poorly	p115
● Finishing weakly	p116

To put together a solid round of golf you have to start and finish well, otherwise you'll always be playing catch-up.

Coping with the conditions

A golf course rarely appears in perfect condition. There is always one element that is playing tricks with the golf ball, whether it is the wind, rain or sun. It is rare to play on the perfect still day.

For this reason, struggling in imperfect conditions will make the sport more difficult. Playing in the wet and hot or cold weather are just part of golfing life. Coping with the conditions is down to preparation.

On-course first aid and long-term recovery

FIXES	GO TO PAGE
● Dealing with wet weather	p117
● Extreme conditions	p117

Coping in the heat is as much a skill as dealing with windy conditions.

You can always make golf a year-round sport by conquering wintry weather.

Dealing with first-tee nerves

First-tee nerves are a good thing. They help sharpen your game and make you alert and ready to go. You will, though, only be able to realize the benefits of nervous, well-channelled, energy, if you have prepared properly before the round.

Quick fixes

Take a confidence club

Give yourself a chance of keeping the ball in play when you are struck with nerves by using your favourite club. This may only be a 5-iron, but hitting 165m (180yd) down the middle sets the round up better than not making it past the red tees. You may be behind your playing partner, but you're more likely to be on the short stuff.

Find your putting rhythm

Rhythm is the key to the perfect putt. Take five minutes on the practice green before you tee off. This will help you to find a putting rhythm for the day. You don't want to work on anything technical; just make some putts until your stroke feels comfortable and relaxed.

Trick yourself into confidence

It is possible to trick yourself into feeling confident by adopting positive and confident body language. However nervous you are feeling, walk on to the first tee with your chest out, your head held high, standing tall and with a determined, confident look on your face. You will soon start to feel the way you look, and it is bound to affect your opponents as well.

Don't walk on to the first tee with your head down on your chest and your shoulders slouched. If you want to feel confident and give off a confident air then walk with your back straight and your head held high.

Following bogeys with bogeys

If you are endlessly following bogeys with bogeys and find yourself caught in an uninspiring spiral of damaging numbers, you need to take time before you tee off to prepare for what's to come.

Quick fix

Play six courses in one

A great way to prepare for a round is to divide the round up into six courses of three holes each. Then look at each mini-course and work out what sort of score you would be happy with over those three holes. If you are a couple over par, put it behind you and concentrate on the next mini-course. Start again, fresh in your mind, because you have not dropped a shot on this new course yet. You will soon find you are picking up shots.

Develop a routine that starts your 'new course'. Shut your eyes, count to twenty and work out what you'll wear tomorrow. Then open your eyes again and start your 'new course' afresh from what has gone before.

BOUNCING TIGER

Tiger Woods is a great exponent of never letting a bad hole get to him. He is consistently leading the 'bounce-back' statistics on the US PGA Tour. This is the stat that tells you how often you make birdie after a bogey. Woods's recovery rate is phenomenal. Try to improve your 'bounce-back' by forgetting about your dropped shots and concentrating on the task in hand.

By dividing your round into manageable chunks, bouncing back becomes easier and you'll drop fewer shots.

Following highs with lows

It is easy to leak shot after shot and it is just as easy to play badly after playing very well. If you are suffering highs and lows in your rounds, you need to rethink your approach.

Quick fix

Staying level-headed

Just as you must never get too despondent after a bad hole, it is disastrous to become too excited after a good one. If you sink a long putt or hit a close short iron, put it behind you and focus on the next shot. The key to consistent golf is staying level and not losing your focus. You have all the time in the world to relive that shot in the clubhouse later.

A great example of this was Howard Clarke during the 1995 Ryder Cup at Oak Hill – and there is no more hyped situation in golf than the Ryder Cup. Clarke holed his tee shot on a par-3 in his crucial match against Peter Jacobsen in the final day's singles match. The crowd went nuts, caddies went mad, commentators screamed. Clarke simply bent down, picked up his tee and walked calmly to the green, with only a deep breath and a quick wave to acknowledge the shot. He went on to win by a hole.

The coolness of a winner is shown not only by keeping calm when things are going badly, but dealing with success with a level head until the job's completed.

Only deal with one shot at a time and do not get ahead of yourself.

Decent scoring comes down to staying level through the highs and the lows.

After a great shot, put it behind you and concentrate on the next one.

Starting poorly

The first hole sets the tone for your round. Feeling confident and unhurried will have an effect on how you play throughout. Decent preparation is the key for hitting the course running.

Quick fixes

Play the first hole before the first hole

To settle first-tee nerves you should give yourself time before you start to hit some balls on the range. This time is not for working on your game; it is for loosening your golf muscles and focusing your mind.

The best preparation you can do pre-round on the range is to play the first hole in your mind at least three times. If you are hitting a driver from the first, then hit a few drivers from the range.

If your approach after a solid drive is usually an 8-iron, then hit a few 8-irons. Do this alternately: hitting driver then 8-iron and going through your pre-shot routine each time. When you are on the first tee, it will feel like your seventh hole and your nerves will have gone.

Starting and finishing your warm-up well

To conclude your warm-up, you should hit some gentle wedges so that you feel the rhythm and tempo of your swing as well as the ball coming off the middle of the club.

On the practice putting green, take 30 seconds to hole three or four small putts in a row. This gives you good positive signals about balls dropping in holes before you start in anger. A positive finish on the practice green leads to a positive start on the tee.

An effective – even if not very long – warm-up can save you numerous shots.

Finishing badly

It is an unfulfilling feeling when you finish badly. If you have done well over 16 holes, stringing together a half-decent score, then letting shots slip down 17 and 18 leaves a very sour taste in the mouth. This is a key segment of the round and it should not be taken lightly.

Quick fix

Finish in style

Of all the key moments in a round of golf, the most crucial are the closing holes, as they ultimately decide what you sign for on your card. There are three problems you need to address over 17 and 18: physical fatigue and low energy; mental fatigue and worsening concentration; and 'job done' syndrome where you feel as though you are already in the bar.

Improve your general level of fitness. Taking regular walks and exercise will help, as will simple things like eating and drinking through the round. Make sure you drink enough fluids and eat foods that release energy quickly, such as bananas.

Make a conscious effort to refocus on the 17th tee as too many cards are ruined on the home straight.

Your round does not finish on the 16th hole. Learning how to finish strongly is crucial to low scoring.

A good standard of physical fitness will help mental fitness and will help to prevent mental fatigue. At this stage in the round, it is crucial to stick to a pre-shot routine. A swing will work well on auto-pilot if you have a decent routine. Stay with your game plan. If you always planned to hit a 3-iron off 18, don't change to a driver in the hope that you might pick up a shot. You won't.

As soon as you have holed out on 16, take five seconds to relax. Forget what has passed and play the last two holes as though it is a separate day. Don't look at your score. Concentrate solely on your closing shots to finish the job professionally.

Dealing with extreme conditions

Playing in wet weather is unpleasant at the best of times but certain golfers, 1999 Open champion Paul Lawrie for one, thrive in the worst conditions. If you follow certain rules, you can play well when the weather's miserable.

To score well in the wet, the crucial element is to keep the grips of the clubs dry. If the grips are dry, you will be able to swing freely. You should also take an extra club for most shots because the ground will be soft and your swing is unlikely to be as fluid as normal. That means you will lose distance.

Quick fixes

Wet weather keys
1 Have some decent waterproofs to hand.

2 Make sure your shoes are waterproofed as there is nothing worse than wet socks.

3 Keep an umbrella up at all times when not playing shots.

4 Have a hood on your bag to keep your clubs dry.

5 Keep a number of towels in your bag.

Adjusting to the heat and the cold
Playing in hot and cold conditions presents different problems and either extreme can be as difficult as the other. Through taking some simple precautions you can save yourself a headache as well as shots.

For both hot and cold conditions, there is one predominant maxim: wear a hat. A hat will keep the heat in during cold weather as more heat is lost through the top of your head than any other part of your body. It also protects you from the sun in hot weather – a golf course, by definition, is an exposed area and the sun is unforgiving. Just remember to wear a woolly hat to cope with the cold and a light hat to protect you from the heat.

The ball also travels further in hot weather, and breaks more on the greens if they are hard and fast, so allow for this when selecting clubs. You will find in colder climes that the ball flies much shorter; just ask those who contest the Drambuie Ice Golf Championship in Greenland each year. So take an extra club to cope with the cold.

Be sensible with what you wear. You don't want to melt in hot weather or freeze in the cold, so wear enough layers to keep comfortable through the round – a comfortable body will always lead to a comfortable swing.

Decent preparation is the key to dealing with extreme weather conditions.

Benefiting from first-tee nerves

First-tee nerves can be debilitating but this nervous energy can also help your game. Top sports stars often say that they perform better when they are slightly nervous because it gets the adrenaline flowing and their senses are heightened. It is the same for golfers. Use your first-tee adrenaline to be confident and positive. Here are four long-term tips that will help channel these forces in the right direction.

Take your time

Give yourself plenty of time before you tee off. Use this time not only to warm up your muscles but also to check that you have everything you need for the first tee: ball, tee, marker, pencil and any other accessory you use. There are few things worse than plunging into your bag on the first fairway to dig out a rusting pitch-mark repairer after you have rushed your tee-shot. Replenish your bag after each round, not before, so you are always prepared for the next time.

Prepare gently

On the first tee, make a conscious effort to slow down your routine. Nerves will naturally speed everything up, so make everything last those few seconds longer as you prepare for the opening shot.

Relax into action

Relax the pressure in your left hand when you grip the club. Nerves tighten muscles, which restricts the fluidity of your swing. Lightening the grip will ease tension and make for a smoother stroke.

Focus fully

Plot the first hole carefully. As you stand on the first tee, think of nothing but how you will conquer that hole. Ignore the chattering crowds waiting to play behind you or the club captain who's just teed off in front. This is your ball, your hole and your game – you know how to play this hole, so stick to your plan and be positive.

There is nothing more off-putting than rushing on to the first tee – take your time.

Have a clear idea of your tactics for the first hole so you can deal with those initial jitters.

Efficient management

Good course management will save you five shots a round. No need to practise, no need to have lessons, no need to hit practice balls; but still five shots saved. Here are the two rules that will save a high-handicap golfer those needlessly wasted strokes.

The seven out of ten rule

When in trouble, stuck in trees or thick rough, and you see the chance to hit the heroic shot, think how many times out of ten you could pull it off. If it is fewer than seven, don't bother. Good scores come from playing percentage golf.

The magic 150m rule

When eyeing up a rescue shot, it is not advisable to try to hit as close to the green as possible, especially if this entails greater risk. All you have to do from a tricky position is get inside that

magic 150m (165yd) mark and on to the fairway. Once you are there, you give yourself a chance. It is sometimes easier to hit close from 100m (110yd) out than to pitch in from that nasty 45m (50yd) range.

Chipping out sideways will save you more shots a round than glory shots will.

If you can pull the shot off seven times out of ten, then go for it.

PRACTICE AND EQUIPMENT

Effective practice

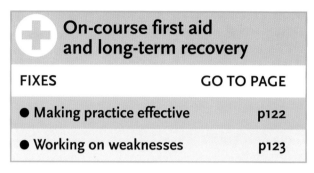

➕ On-course first aid and long-term recovery

FIXES	GO TO PAGE
● Making practice effective	p122
● Working on weaknesses	p123

Amateur golfers often pop down to the range, buy 100 balls and get through 100 drives in double-quick time. They then complain that they are not improving, despite the hours and money spent on the range.

To make practice effective you must focus on quality, and not quantity. Although amateurs are unlikely to spend hours on the range honing their skills, there are some basic principles that could make all the difference to your game. People think that practice makes perfect, but practice makes permanent is more accurate. So if you are practising a faulty swing then your faults will be harder to rectify. Hence the importance of quality practice.

Practising badly is as damaging to your game as swinging badly. Develop a quality practice routine.

Manufacturing scores

Equipment manufacturers would have you believe that you can buy a good game. The newest driver, the best ball will automatically turn you into a single-figure-handicap golfer. There is, without doubt, a kernel of truth in this but it is not quite the one that the equipment advertisements convey.

You must be able to swing the club proficiently before you can make use of any technological advancements – you would not buy a Ferrari if you couldn't drive – but having equipment suited to your game is an invaluable help to shaving shots off your card.

BEWARE THE PLACEBO EFFECT

Often when a golfer uses new equipment, their game feels reinvented. The ball whizzes off the face of an expensive driver like a firework. They pay (lots) and walk home a transformed golfer. Then the effect of the new club wears off and old swing faults start to haunt ball flight – the placebo effect.

A new piece of equipment can boost confidence and be exciting, leading to better ball-striking. But as soon as the confidence wanes, the slice returns. Do not be tricked by a few good shots, a label and a hefty price tag. Make sure the club suits you before you pay.

✚ On-course first aid and long-term recovery

FIXES	GO TO PAGE
● Equipped for success	p124
● Getting a grip	p125
● Lies	p125
● Club shafts	p125

Effective practice

It is a common problem with amateur golfers that they hit balls aimlessly on the driving range without a technical thought between their ears. This is great exercise but it will not improve your game. Try these practice hints to make the most of your golf work-out.

Quick fixes

Check alignment
So many faults originate from faulty alignment at address. When you are working on your swing, you can keep a continual check on alignment by placing a club along the ground parallel to your target line. It does not matter what element, or what shot, you are working on, you can never work hard enough on good alignment.

Pick a target
Instead of hitting aimlessly down the range, pick out a target at which to fire. This may be a pin near the 150m (165yd) marker, a tree in the distance or a silly landmark, such as a cardboard Mickey Mouse. Whenever you hit a ball, have a target. On the course, you hit a shot at a target so practice should replicate the real thing.

Less is more
Hit fewer balls and have more practice swings – for each shot you hit, run through your pre-shot routine so that it becomes second nature. Any low-handicap or professional golfer finds it more difficult to forget their routine than remember it.

Effective practice means quality not quantity, so work out a practice strategy to get the most from your sessions.

DON'T KID YOUR PRO

Many amateur golfers will start trying to improve their swing when they have booked a lesson or if the pro is passing, offering some friendly advice. This is madness – like seeing a doctor because you feel ill and pretending nothing is wrong. Be honest with the pro and you'll get the most out of them. Most of the game is played around the green, but golfers rarely go for short game lessons. In just one session, you could improve your green play enormously.

Work on weaknesses

Many golfers who hit the ball a long way will stand on the range doing just that: hitting the ball a long way. If you can already do it and are confident with a driver, this will not improve your game. Instead, target your weaknesses in your practice sessions. Leave at home the clubs with which you are confident. Plan a practice week, devoting time to all areas of the game.

Practise your putting 50 per cent of the time

The putter is the club that you use the most in a round yet it is probably the club with which you practice least. This makes no sense.

A mirror can be a great tool to check posture, alignment and positions in your swing.

A MIRROR IMAGE

If you get the chance, check your set-up and posture in front of a mirror. Most problems with the golf swing come from a mistake at address and the mirror will give you instant answers as to where the problems lie. This tool can also be used to check parts of the swing itself, such as swing plane, and whether you retain your spine angle throughout.

Devote as much of your time to developing a consistent, positive putting stroke as to developing a consistent swing. There are hundreds of putting drills and games that can make practising fun. It is much better to use one of these than to putt aimlessly for an hour. Give it some focus. Even better, ask your local professional for a putting lesson.

When it comes to practice, each of us is different. Every golfer has their own pain or boredom threshold. Some can beat balls to the early hours, while others shiver at the sight of a full bucket.

Having individual practice routines is as true for the professional game as it is for the amateur. There are the grinders – Vijay Singh and Padraig Harrington – and the more leisurely golfers. Colin Montgomerie treats practice sessions as warm-ups and fine-tuning. The lesson from this is simple: do as much practice as suits your temperament. If you practise for the sake of it, then stop. You will not improve and are less likely to enjoy it.

Equipped for success

Every top golfer has had clubs specially fitted for them. They may look like standard ones but the manufacturers have tweaked and adjusted them so that they fit the golfer perfectly.

Too many amateur golfers let their swing fit the equipment when it should be the other way round – the clubs should suit the golfer. If you are 195cm tall (6ft 6in), you are not going to enjoy playing with standard-length shafts because they will leave you reaching for the ball. If you are 165cm tall (5ft 5in), you don't want to play with clubs that come up to your shoulders.

Some golfers swing aggressively; others are more rhythmical. Different types of swing need different shafts. There are numerous variations on shafts and if you are playing with shafts that are not suitable for you, you will not find the consistency your swing merits. Ask your local professional to look at your swing and advise on custom-fitting.

Find the right shaft to suit you and you will improve your scores without even hitting a ball.

Sizing up equipment

There are four parts of the golf club that can have a massive effect on the ball flight: the clubhead; the grip; the lie angle; and the shaft.

The clubhead

The clubhead is the part of the club that attracts the most attention. It has two main attributes that will affect performance: aesthetics and feel. If you don't like the look of a club – it may be too thin, too fat, too round, too square or just plain ugly, then you are unlikely to swing with much confidence. Similarly, if, when you make contact, the clubhead feels heavy or rigid, you may swing more hesitantly. When you are choosing irons or woods, bear both of these factors in mind as they will affect the performance you get from the equipment much more than any promotional blurb or price tag. Everyone has individual tastes.

Oversize drivers have moved from being fashionable accessories in a golf bag to becoming an essential part of modern equipment. Contrary to common belief, they do not make you hit the ball much further than an old-fashioned driver. There is a small improvement in length but the greatest difference oversize drivers make is in their forgiveness. The face of the club is so large that it's harder to mis-hit the shot than to hit it well.

| 6-iron | 8-iron | pitching-wedge | driver |

Modern equipment has made the game easier, so take advantage of technology.

Bad shots that would not have got airborne with a small-headed driver, fly 250m (280yd) straight down the middle. Slices are straighter, hooks less vicious and the game more accessible. If you don't have a new driver in your bag, you are at a disadvantage – the workman can be helped by his tools.

The grip
If you have a grip that is too thin for your hands, you may find that there is too much hand action in your swing. This could lead to nasty hooks as you lose control of the clubhead through impact. If the grip is too thick, your hand action may be restricted and this will lead to blocks and slices because you will be unable to release the club properly through the hitting zone.

Your grip is too thin if you find that the fingers on your left hand press into your palm when you address the ball. Your grip is too thick if there is a gap between the fingers and palm of your left hand at address. Your fingers on your left hand should touch your palm lightly at address – this is the correct width of grip.

The lie angle
When the club's lie is too upright, the heel will strike the turf first and could cause the club to close at impact, sending the ball left. If the lie is too flat, the opposite happens, with the toe catching the ground first and spinning the ball out right. The lie of the club is too flat if the clubhead's heel is in the air at address. It is too upright if the toe is in the air – the club should lie flat to the ground. So use clubs that give you a decent, flat, lie angle.

The shaft
Shafts are the engines of the club. Many professional golfers feel they are the most important part. Visit a professional who will advise you on the correct shaft for your swing. Amateurs often feel they need a stiffer shaft than they do – a common misconception – only the best golfers swing fast enough to benefit from a stiff-shafted club. If you play with a regular shaft, it is easier to get the ball airborne and you will have more control over the ball's flight. So allow yourself to be guided by expert advice.

Index

Acknowledgements

Author's acknowledgements

Many thanks to Anna Legge for feeding, nursing and
inspiring me at Tidelines. More thanks than I can muster
to the entire 'Golf Monthly' team, both immediate past
and present, for making my work read well and look good.

Publishers' acknowledgements

Executive Editor Trevor Davies
Editor Jessica Cowie
Executive Art Editor Peter Burt, Karen Sawyer
Designers Anthony Cohen, Colin Goody
Illustration Axos
Picture Research Jennifer Veall
Production Controller Ian Paton

Picture credits

Octopus Publishing Group Limited/Mark Newcombe 4-5,
6 left, 6-7, 7 right, 8 left, 8 right, 8 centre, 9 left, 9 centre,
11 left, 11 right, 12 left, 13 left, 13 right, 15, 16 left, 16 right,
17 right, 20, 21 left, 21 right, 22, 24 left, 24 right, 26, 28 left,
28 right, 28 centre, 29 left, 29 right, 29 centre, 31 left, 31 right,
33 left, 33 right, 35 left, 35 right, 35 centre left, 35 centre right,
36 left, 36 right, 36 centre left, 36 centre right, 37 left, 37 right,
39 top, 39 bottom, 41 left, 42 left, 42 right, 42 centre, 45 right,
47 left, 48 left, 48 right, 49 left, 49 right, 50, 51 left, 51 right,
51 centre, 52 left, 52 centre, 53 top right, 53 bottom right, 53
bottom left, 60, 60 right, 61, 62 right, 62 centre, 64 left, 64
centre, 65 left, 65 centre, 66, 68 top, 68 bottom right, 68
bottom left, 69 top, 69 bottom right, 69 bottom left, 72 left,
72 right, 74 right, 74 centre, 75 left, 77, 78, 79 left, 79 right,
80 top left, 80 bottom left, 81 left, 81 right, 81 centre, 82 top,
82 bottom right, 82 bottom left, 83 bottom, 84 left, 84 right,
85 left, 85 right, 85 centre, 87 top right, 87 bottom left, 88, 89
bottom right, 89 bottom centre, 92, 93, 94, 97, 98 left, 98
right, 98 centre, 99 left, 99 right, 99 centre, 103 left, 103 right,
103 centre left, 103 centre right, 104 right, 104 centre, 105 left,
105 right, 105 centre, 108, 109 top, 110, 111 right, 113, 114 left,
114 right, 114 centre, 115, 118, 119 left, 120, 121, 124 left, 124
right, 125/Nick Walker 2-3, 9 right, 10, 12 right, 17 left, 25 right,
32 left, 32 right, 32 centre, 34, 44 left, 44 right, 45 left, 47 right,
52 right, 54, 57 left, 57 right, 57 centre, 58 left, 58 right, 59 left,
59 right, 59 centre, 70 left, 70 right, 80 top right, 80 centre
right, 80 bottom right, 83 top centre, 83 top left, 83 top right,
86, 89 top centre, 95 left, 95 right, 100 left, 100 right, 100
centre, 102 left, 102 right, 102 centre left, 102 centre right,
104 centre left, 104 bottom left, 111 left, 118 right, 119 right
Phil Sheldon 117